CyberMeeting

CyberMeeting

How to Link People and Technology in Your Organization

James L. Creighton
James W. R. Adams

AMACOM
American Management Association
New York • Atlanta • Boston • Chicago • Kansas City • San Francisco • Washington, D.C.
Brussels • Mexico City • Tokyo • Toronto

This publication is designed to provide accurate and authoritative
information in regard to the subject matter covered. It is sold with
the understanding that the publisher is not engaged in rendering legal,
accounting, or other professional service. If legal advice or other expert
assistance is required, the services of a competent professional person
should be sought.

Library of Congress Cataloging-in-Publication Data

Creighton, James L.
    CyberMeeting : how to link people and technology in your
    organization / James L. Creighton, James W. R. Adams.
        p.   cm.
    Includes index.
    ISBN 0-8144-0352-2
    1. Videoconferencing.   2. Groupware.   3. Scheduling—Computer
    programs.   I. Adams, James W. R.   II. Title.
    HF5734.7.C73   1997
    658.4'5—DC21
                                                    97–22979
                                                    CIP

Printing number

10 9 8 7 6 5 4 3 2 1

To my mother,
Helen Creighton,
who fostered a deep love
for books and reading

and

To my wife,
Lucy Adams,
in grateful appreciation
for her unflagging
encouragement and support

Contents

Preface

Over the next decade organizations will spend billions connecting their employees through technology that will permit collaboration and electronic participation in meetings. Many organizations will find new ways of working together that give them a competitive edge in every aspect of their operations. Hundreds of millions of those dollars will be wasted chasing fads and installing technology that people will use to work the same way they worked before the technology was installed.

This book is about how to manage the transition to cyber-collaboration so that your organization gets full advantage of its investment. Because we are all walking a new path and the technology seems to be changing daily, there is no single right answer for how your organization should proceed. The authors hope to provide the basic information you need to have, raise the key issues, and ask the right questions. Each organization will necessarily have to find its own path to making meetings more effective.

This book is about making meetings and other forms of collaboration effective organization-wide. Meeting technology is one way to do that, but we think there are others that are equally important. We do believe that technology creates a tremendous potential for synergies among all the approaches to collaboration that would otherwise not exist.

This is not a guide about how to improve a particular meeting, although you may pick up a number of ideas along the way. It's also not a guide to running electronic meetings.

In a few years there will be enough lore to provide guidelines on how to run a cybermeeting. The authors may even want to write such a book. But, at this point, it would be a very short book indeed. Most of the advice would be based on what we know about how to make meetings more effective now.

Most organizations are not completely utilizing the full range of innovations that are currently available. So there is plenty that can be done to improve meeting effectiveness right now, before your organization installs new technology.

Our book provides sufficient technical information so that managers can understand the important choices. We have avoided describing the attributes of specific hardware or software for the simple reason that this information becomes quickly obsolete. There would be no surer guarantee that this book would have a shelf life of just a few hours than to provide a briefing on specific technology.

We come to interest in collaborative technologies from different paths. Jim Creighton is President of Creighton & Creighton, Inc., Los Gatos, California (www.CandCInc.com), and has been an independent consultant for nearly 30 years. He has designed and facilitated hundreds of meetings, workshops, conferences, and team building and strategic planning sessions. He is particularly known for designing processes for including the public in major public policy issues, and for building consensus on difficult technical issues. His interest in collaborative technologies grew out of a generalized interest in how to expand participation in decision making, but more specifically out of managing an interactive meeting center for the U.S. Department of Labor. This center, described in more detail in Chapter Six, provided a residence for teams of Labor Department employees working on new legislation, policies, or proposed rules. Teams were housed in the facilities for several weeks or even several months, with 2–3 teams in residence at the same time. The center included meeting space and workstations, with everyone in the facility linked on the most advanced groupware of the time, Lotus Notes. Creighton & Creighton staff not only ran the everyday operations of the center but also provided facilitation, team building, and other kinds of organizational consulting. Jim Creighton was inspired by this experience to explore the potential of combining the best of technology with the best of group process and organizational development expertise, all in the best possible facility. Writing *CyberMeeting* was his way of explaining how these can best be combined.

Jim Adams comes to collaborative technology through the perspective of someone who has introduced and managed collaborative processes in large organizations, and designs and uses meeting facilities. He is currently Senior Vice President, Development, for Madison Square Garden, where he is introducing many of the technologies discussed in this book. Previously he was a member of the Viacom/Paramount Technology Council and helped lead the corporation into the interactive media business. He was a major contributor to the research and planning that led to Viacom's entry into the on-line services business. He was also responsible for the design and development of an interactive sports program pilot for both the on-line services and interactive television markets. Previously, Adams organized the project team charged with designing and constructing the Disney theme park in France. This followed a career in the U.S. Army Corps of Engineers, during which he served as District Engineer, Jacksonville District, and was Deputy Chief of Staff, Engineer, for the U.S. Army Training and Doctrine Command, with an annual budget of $1 billion.

We met through a shared interest in dispute resolution while Adams was still with the Corps of Engineers, an organization for which Jim Creighton has served as a consultant for many years. They have shared ideas and worked together on occasional projects for the past 15 years.

With this background, the authors find it impossible to think about collaborative technology without thinking about all the aspects of organizational life that play a role in how people within organizations collaborate. Their goal is to approach collaboration as a system in which collaborative technology plays an important integrating role but is just part of the answer to helping people work together more effectively.

Acknowledgments

From Jim Creighton's perspective, the genesis of this book was running a "skunkworks," a highly interactive meeting facility housing temporary teams working on crash projects, for the Department of Labor. The skunkworks, known more formally as The Policy Center, brought together many of the elements of this book: facility design, groupware technology, group process, and corporate culture, all in the service of improving team productivity. Although it was only a precursor of the meeting facilities described in this book, it inspired new thinking about what could be.

Secretary of Labor Robert Reich was the instigator for the skunkworks, with Deputy Assistant Secretary Roland Droitsch responsible for overseeing implementation. Jim Jones and Mark Hunker both played a key role in supporting the operations of the center. Maggie Creighton set up and managed the overall operation of the center on behalf of Creighton & Creighton, Inc. Rich Cooper and Tim Fuller ably staffed the center, at times nearly a 24-hour-a-day operation. Jim Channon, Langdon Morris, Paul Grabhorn, and Bill Robertson all provided creative ideas on how to improve the center.

Jim Adams's interest in collaborative technology has been long-standing, but was restimulated by his commitment to keeping Madison Square Garden the world's leading venue for public events. The operation of Madison Square Garden is always time-pressured, requiring incredible coordination and commitment. We salute the remarkable people at Madison Square Garden who make collaborative efforts a high art form.

Many people contributed generously of their time by giving us ideas or reviewing drafts of the book. Our special thanks to: Fred Litto, a leading investigator of collaborative technology at the University of São Paulo, Brazil, for his friendship, and for periodic visits in which he insists on finding out the latest on what's new and creative; Joe Okinori Ouye, President of Facility Technics, for many suggestions, a perceptive review, and for opening doors; Jan Dekema, President of Stratiquest, Inc., for sharing insights into his research on collaborative technology for a consortium of high-tech firms; Ann Bamesberger, of Sun Microsystems, for sharing her research on the impact of facilities upon productivity; J. Bruce Harreld, Senior Vice President, Strategy, and Bob Boss, World Wide Director of Telecommunications, IBM Corporation, for sharing their insights about future directions in collaborative technoloy, and for reviewing the book; Michelle Pitcher of PictureTel, for providing the equivalent of a post-graduate education in videoconferencing; Jim Channon, for sharing his drawings and stimulating thoughts about the design of "50 square miles of virtual reality"; Langdon Morris, for sharing his drawings of possible floorplans for the U.S. Department of Labor Skunkworks; David Sibbett for sharing examples of his "group guides"; Andre Delbecq, a distinguished researcher on innovation in high-technology companies, for his insightful review of the manuscript; Ken Cannizaro, who's held a number of senior executive positions with high-tech companies, for his thoughtful and supportive review of the manuscript; the 3M Corporation, for permission to quote from studies it funded at the Wharton Center for Applied Research and Annenberg School for Communication (and to Lynn Oppenheim and Peter Monge, the principal researchers for those studies); John Christofano and Lori-Leanne Parris, for their insights on Silicon Graphic's intranet; Gail Taylor, Matt Taylor, Patsy Kahoe, Colonel Bill Rutley, and Amelia Tess Thornton, for insights on MG Taylor's DesignShops; Gayle Pergamit and Chris Peterson, who gave us the opportunity to read and take material from their forthcoming book about MG Taylor; and Roland Droitsch, Deputy Assistant Secretary of Labor, for correcting the factual errors in our description of the U.S. Department of Labor Skunkworks, and for his unflagging support of the Skunkworks in the face of budget cuts and bureaucratic inertia.

Special thanks go to Laurie Harper of Sebastian Literary Agency, who stuck with us through thick and thin, providing warm support and thoughtful suggestions. Many thanks also to the staff of AMACOM for believing in the book and bringing it to market at breakneck speed.

Finally, to Maggie Creighton and Lucy Adams for putting up with us throughout, and continuing to love us in spite of it.

Jim Creighton   Jim Adams
Los Gatos, Calif.   New York, N.Y.

CyberMeeting

1

Cybermeetings

It's the year 2005 at FutureTech, Inc. It's a typically busy day managing the company's far-flung international operations, and many of the staff of FutureTech are in meetings. But FutureTech's meetings look just a little bit different:

> John Rogers, the vice president of engineering, needs to discuss a report on a suspected flaw in a digital control chip. He sends all participants an e-mail message asking them to read the report and be prepared to discuss it this afternoon. Some of the individuals John wants to talk to are in the same building, but others are located in other time zones. Some participants will need to participate from their laptop computers at home, or in transit.
>
> Because it's an urgent meeting, the e-mail message shows up as a yellow stickie on everyone's screen. John schedules the meeting by having his **software agent** communicate directly with agents for the other participants. These agents are authorized to schedule meetings with anyone on an approved list. So when John's agent contacts them, the agents all work together to find a convenient time for all. These software agents can even initiate phone calls to track down people away from their offices.
>
> A few people decide to join John in his office, but most work directly at the screen on the PC in their office. Once everybody is in place, the screen shows the report and live-action video of each participant (taken by miniature cameras mounted on each participant's PC). Participants type in pro-

posed changes that everyone can see on their own screen. People can respond verbally, or by typing in alternative proposals. Once the changes are agreed upon, each participant saves the file and prints out a copy on his or her own printer.

Within an hour, the problem has been defined, a solution identified, and an implementation plan determined.

The advantages of such meetings should be immediately obvious. Even if a meeting has to be scheduled, nobody had to do the arduous task of scheduling a mutually acceptable time for busy people. No one has to travel from Hong Kong, or Korea, to attend the meeting. In fact, people don't even have to leave their offices. The only time spent is the time of actual discussion. Yet each participant can see the other participants, getting the benefit not only of their words, but of body language and facial expressions.

CYBERMEETING INNOVATIONS

○ Use of software agents to schedule meetings

○ Desktop videoconferencing

○ Use of groupware to work simultaneously on a single product or even multiple projects

---

Many meetings require intense face-to-face interaction over many hours or even days. Here's another meeting going on at FutureTech today:

Roseann's new project team is starting a 2-month crash process to identify new products. There are ten members of her core team, six representing different functions within FutureTech, two representing FutureTech suppliers, one representing a major FutureTech customer, plus Roseann. In addition, there are four other team members with special expertise who will participate in key meetings, but who will do so from their distant locations. Finally, there are literally dozens of FutureTech personnel and many suppliers who are vitally concerned about the decisions the team will make, who need to be consulted throughout the process.

During the 2 months, Roseann's entire team will be housed at the FutureTech Meetings Center. This is a special facility designed to provide both human and technical support for effective meetings. The reason for housing all the core team in a single place is to build a strong sense of team identity. Also, being housed together encourages the informal interaction that often is most crucial in coming up with breakthrough ideas for new products. During the time that the team will be in the Meetings Center there will be other FutureTech groups holding meetings at the Center. The social areas in the Center, where coffee and refreshments are available at all times, are designed to encourage interaction between the groups. Some of the best ideas happen serendipitously when people from different groups are chatting over a cup of coffee.

Every aspect of the Center can be modified to support the objectives of the people using it. Meeting spaces can be almost instantly reconfigured to accommodate meetings of from 4 to 200 people. Lighting and sound can be regulated to create supportive moods. Noise suppression technology can be employed so that a number of meetings can go on at the same time without participants' being bothered by noise. If security is an issue, spaces can be prepared that permit full protection from electronic eavesdropping. Each member of the team has a workstation in the Center, with the latest computer equipment, groupware for all team members, and teleconferencing capability back to his or her home office using minicameras mounted on PCs. People participating in meetings receive full clerical support from Meetings Center staff who provide word processing, copying, and message taking support. Specialists at the Center can also prepare graphics and maps, produce multimedia presentations, and produce reports.

Because their projects are of high priority, the core team will have exclusive use of their work space for the time they are in the Center. Some of the other occupants of the Center have been assigned spaces on a "hotelling" basis. That is, they are given full use of a workstation, but if they are gone for a few days the Center staff will store their work materials in special storage lockers. With a few hours' notice, their office will be set up to go again, right down to the nameplate on the door.

Prior to the meeting, Roseann meets with a **meeting systems specialist** from the Center and together they develop a preliminary contract for the services the team will receive from the Center. Roseann requests help from a professional **meeting facilitator** for all major team meetings. She also requests the support of a **meeting technician** to handle all the electronic and telephonic systems that the team will be using. In addition to handling the technology, the meeting technician's job is to assist with presentations and prepare a summary of meetings.

As they enter the room for their first meeting, team members are immediately drawn to the colorful murals that cover the walls from floor to ceiling. As the facilitator opens the meeting, the murals fade, and reveal **working walls** and presentation screens. The working walls are actually covered with a **thin film** that allows the walls to be used as an electronic slate, recording everything written on the walls and displaying everything received from a computer operated by the meeting technician. One entire wall is a high-definition flat-screen television monitor. Different members of the team—one in Tokyo, one in Germany, one in Singapore, and one (a world-class designer who works only from her home) in Maui—are displayed in each quadrant of the screen. At each seat there is a computer keyboard and monitor set into the table. At each seat there is also an electronic slate people can use to make freehand drawings and write ideas. Anything typed on the keyboard or drawn on the slate can be projected onto the walls.

As each member of the team introduces himself/herself, a photo of the team member, plus his or her title and a brief synopsis of experience, is projected onto one of the working walls. Team members who want more information about any of the others can pull up brief résumés by selecting from the menu on the computer console built into the table for each participant. Team members need not have exceptional training to perform these technological feats. The technology is handled by the meeting technician, who also plays a brief orientation video showing members how to handle their end of the meeting room technology.

After explaining the purpose of today's meeting, and laying out ground rules, the facilitator calls on Roseann, the team leader, to set out the overall goals for the team. Roseann's presentation is projected automatically onto the wall. Her presentation includes brief video comments from the CEO laying out the goals of the project and explaining how it fits into company strategy. Time has been scheduled later in the day so that the CEO can talk with the team from his office, by direct video connection, after the team has had time to identify questions it would like him to address. As Roseann makes her presentation, team members are able to type questions on their tabletop computers, and these questions then appear on the wall. These include questions from the four remote sites.

An excited discussion follows Roseann's presentation. As the discussion goes on, the meeting technician, using a computer or slate, captures comments in a "visual group memory" shown on the wall. She uses software that lets her quickly draw connections between ideas by means of prepackaged meeting graphics that display related ideas in physical proximity on the wall. She can also use the software to select cartoonlike illustrations or other graphic elements. The group memory begins to grow to cover an entire wall. At one point, an excited team member says, "No, that's in the wrong place." Grabbing a special pen, he walks to the wall and draws a circle around the object he wants moved. He instructs the wall orally to "move this [the circled figure] here," and touches the place on the wall where he would like it to go. The presentation computer, responding to his voice commands, moves the figure to the designated place on the wall. Remote participants are also able to manipulate the material on the wall, by drawing on the screen of the desktop computer built into the table for each participant.

During the meeting, the discussion becomes heated as two team members argue over the potential markets for new products. The facilitator summarizes their positions, then pulls up a menu (on the wall) of databases that can be accessed by the team. Soon the issue about markets is resolved, based upon research findings that were accessed by computer and projected onto the wall in graphic form. In one case, there is an important follow-up question that cannot be immediately answered from the database. The meeting technician sends an e-mail message directly from the room to an individual in the research department in Chicago. A few minutes later, there is an electronic Post-it note on the wall announcing that a response is now available. At an appropriate moment the facilitator asks that the material be shown, and two graphics from the researcher in Chicago are displayed on the wall.

The meeting room technology is designed to support a variety of group processes. For example, when the team is ready for brainstorming on possible new products, the facilitator draws on one of several preprogrammed processes for brainstorming. The computer projects images onto the screen, with accompanying instructions, that lead the team through a process that uses analogies and other stimuli to increase creativity. A voice intones, "A [desired product] is like a tree, a living system . . . " Accompanying the voice is a set of projected images on the walls showing various characteristics of living systems like trees. Team members begin to play with these concepts, applying them to their desired product. Once again, the meeting technician records team members' ideas on the wall, and team members are able to add ideas by typing them in on their computers or writing them on individual electronic slates. As the team runs out of ideas based on the living systems analogy, the facilitator moves on to another stage in the program: "If you could suspend the laws of nature, how would this product work?" This stimulates another round of ideas, with the team eventually addressing how it could produce some of the same features with existing or near-future technology.

Ultimately the team identifies a series of product alternatives that deserve further evaluation and market research. At this point, the facilitator displays a set of alternative planning or development process templates. The templates are simply organizing tools that allow the team to select quickly an overall planning or development process. Each template displays graphically a progression of basic planning or development steps, with space for the team to fill in all the tasks necessary to carry out those basic steps.

The team selects one of the templates, and the template expands to fill an entire wall. Soon the team is gathered at the wall and, using special electronic pens, writing ideas on the wall. All written ideas are instantly scanned and included in the electronic display. This permits people to move items around on the display, or make duplicates of repetitive tasks that appear in a number of steps. The four long-distance participants can also participate since the wall display is also displayed on their computers, and they can make entries that show up on the wall in the Meetings Center. Soon the team has not only identified a number of product options deserving further study, but has also roughed in a plan for how this additional study will be conducted.

Because so many others within FutureTech, as well as some suppliers and major customers, are interested, each night a summary of the meeting is available by modem to anyone with appropriate access codes. Around the world, people throughout the company who are interested in product development come to work and find a note in their e-mail telling them there is a report from Roseann's product development team on the team's intranet home page. People who are interested can access this information at several levels of information. They can pull up a short written summary; they can pull up a summary of all the visual displays, including the brainstorming lists and completed template; or they can pull up the visual group memory summary of the entire group discussion.

Because of time zone differences, people at corporate offices throughout the world have an opportunity to review and comment on the team's work by the time the team reassembles the next morning. Review comments can be transmitted as faxes or e-mail. A few reviewers even attach video comments. This way, the team gets immediate feedback and can make course corrections almost immediately when someone spots a fatal flaw or makes a useful suggestion.

CYBERMEETING INNOVATIONS

○ Meetings held in an interactive meeting center with full electronic support and with interactive social areas

○ Meeting technicians and meeting systems specialists

○ Working walls that record information from individual computers, electronic slates, drawing, and voice command, and that can be downloaded into individual computers

○ Internet and intranet access from meeting room so participants can draw on organizational database, external databases and experts

○ Use of "visual group memory" to record meeting discussion

○ Ability to move material around on the working walls using voice or mouse commands

○ Use of group guides or process wizards to provide structure for planning or decision-making processes

○ Opportunities for people other than team members to receive information from the meeting at the level of information they

> desire, and then be able to send comments to the project team
>
> Other Innovations That Have Been Around Awhile
>
> ○ Including suppliers and customers in product design team
>
> ○ Housing the project team in a meeting center
>
> ○ Use of facilitation
>
> ○ Use of structured group processes for brainstorming

Roseann's team meeting was a full-fledged meeting, using virtually every meeting technology to ensure that the team works productively. But not all meetings look like a meeting. Elsewhere in the building another kind of cybermeeting is taking place in an employee lounge. Neither of the participants thinks of it as a meeting, but its consequences turn out to be as important to FutureTech as what occurs in the scheduled meetings:

> Five years ago when the company built its new facility, it decided that it wanted to encourage informal interaction across organizational lines. So it designed a series of employee lounges, carefully located at those places in the building that adjoined several departments. That way, people from those different departments would bump into each other in the lounges.
>
> In some ways these lounges resemble extremely comfortable coffeehouses, complete with espresso machines, tables, soft chairs, and reading materials. However, a glance around the room shows that there is some serious business equipment here as well. There are several computers that are available

for general use. There's a fax machine/printer and several whiteboards. In fact, there's even one table, an "experimental table" that's just being tried out, where the tabletop is actually a computerized whiteboard. This is the computer age equivalent of the back of an envelope or the tablecloth on which people sketch their ideas.

Bob, who is a senior manufacturing manager, sits down at a table with Gail, who is a design engineer in another department. They were both members of a project team several years back, but have not seen each other in months. Over coffee and tea they catch up with each other and begin talking about the work they are doing now. Gail describes a major design problem that has them stumped. Bob says that reminds him of a manufacturing problem they had awhile back. It was not the same problem exactly, but he vaguely remembers that they found a solution that dealt with some of the same issues. Bob then steps over to an open computer and finds his department's home page on the intranet. He types in a few key words, and the computer gives him a menu of ten files related to those words. In the second file Bob finds what he wants and directs the machine to fax copies of the file to the fax machine in the lounge.

Soon Bob and Gail are poring over the pages. Gail then moves over to the whiteboard and says, "Although it's not an exact fit, maybe if we reversed these steps in the process. . . ." Soon Gail and Bob have sketched out a preliminary approach and print out the drawing on the whiteboard, saving the file back to their respective home workstations. They both agree that they need more expertise. They type some more key words into the computer, which identifies three FutureTech employees with experience in the use of this process. One is in the building, but the other two are at manufacturing plants in other parts of the world. They agree on a list of participants for a desktop videoconference meeting and send it to their software agents to be scheduled for tomorrow. As they leave the lounge they suddenly realize they have been there for almost 2 hours. But they are both excited by the prospect that they may have saved months in getting a new product to market.

CYBERMEETING INNOVATIONS

○ Facilities designed to encourage informal interaction

○ Facilities to augment social interaction, with full electronic support: computer, fax, printer, and whiteboard table

○ Intranet access from places in the building where people socialize

---

Putting the *Cyber* in Cybermeetings

Cybermeetings may sound incredibly futuristic. Yet almost all of the technology described already exists or is currently under development in some laboratory (except for the wall covered with a thin film that serves as a PC-connected whiteboard). Many of the elements are already in use at leading-edge organizations around the world. All of the applications of technology are extensions of approaches already in use by the most progressive organizations to stimulate creativity and increase meeting effectiveness. The three foregoing examples do serve to highlight most of the ingredients of cybermeetings.

In the language of the computer world, the John Rogers's meeting took place in the **desktop environment.** In the desktop environment, meetings are conducted over individual PCs, with the monitor on the PC (or a television) displaying the picture. (We use the term *PC* broadly to include both the Wintel—Microsoft Windows + Intel—and Macintosh machines.) If there is a need to show a real-time picture of an object or person, this is accomplished with a small camera mounted on the PC. One of the goals is to have everybody work together collaboratively but avoid "official" meetings.

Roseann's meeting was held in the **meeting room envi-**

ronment. It might also be called a team room or even a **skunkworks** (more on that later). Here everything is scaled up so that the videoconference viewing screens seem life-size, and work is performed on large meeting room walls. This approach assumes that meetings attended by real people will continue to have value, so the challenge is to make them productive.

Bob and Gail's meeting took place in **informal space.** As we will see, many companies are discovering that in loosely knit, flatter organizations, facilities need to be designed to encourage informal interaction not only within teams but across organizational lines. This is particularly true for knowledge workers, as many innovations occur because of chance conversations between people who—unknown to each other—have information or ideas that address each other's problems.

But what makes these meetings "cyber"? The term *cyber* comes from the field of cybernetics,* a field of study that has produced dramatic breakthroughs in servomechanisms and automation. The public associates the word *cyber* with some kind of human and machine interaction—as in *cyberspace.* We use it that way as well. The innovations we propose in cyber-meetings do involve interactions between humans and machines. Most of them assume the utilization of sophisticated new information technologies.

But it is human/machine interaction we are discussing, not just information technology. Corporate culture and interpersonal conflicts both can block the effective use of new information technologies. Information technology whose design is based on old assumptions about how people can and should work together may constrain rather than support greater productivity. The challenge is to create a synergy between more effective ways of working together and the supporting technology. The primary limit on how cybertechnology will be

---

* The term *cybernetics* was coined by mathematician Norbert Wiener in 1946. Wiener took the name from the Greek word *kyberbetes*, which means "steersman." He used the term to describe an interdisciplinary approach to the study of control and communication in animals, humans, machines, and organizations.

used is human imagination. The FutureTech meetings above only illustrate possibilities rather than predict the way it will be.

Meetings—whether conducted in a formal meeting room, electronically, or over a cup of coffee—are the focal point for interaction in an organization. Meetings bring together people from different parts of the organization (or from different organizations) to communicate, allocate work, resolve disputes, and make decisions. The term *cybermeeting* symbolizes new ways of integrating information technology with innovations in management and group process to produce more effective forms of collaboration. And it could not have come a minute too soon.

2

Meeting Meltdown

All organizations need better communication among employees—who are often geographically separated from one another—and with customers. They also have an urgent need to eliminate wasteful spending associated with traditional, time-consuming meetings. After all, managers are already spending from 25% to 65% of their time in meetings.

Anybody old enough to remember air travel before the 1970s will recall that every ticket had to be written by hand. All reservations were made by phone with each individual airline. If there were reservations involving more than one airline, the clerk would have to phone the other airline to complete the reservation. Almost all seat assignments were made at the gate, with frequent duplication of assignments. Some airlines even made up silhouettes of each plane with little stickers for each seat that were then put on the boarding pass so that the sticker could not be duplicated. Sometimes the system even worked.

The reality is that—with more than three times as many domestic passenger miles flown in 1995 as in 1970—air travel as we know it could not have occurred without the computer. Had the same demand occurred with the old reservation system, the system would have collapsed under its own weight.

Changes in Nature and Frequency of Meetings

The new collaborative technologies discussed in Chapter One are also arriving just in time. These new technologies offer a critical set of tools to companies that must deal with a number of important trends that their predecessors did not have had to face:

- ○ Shorter cycle times for product development
- ○ Global, not just national, competitors
- ○ Decision-making authority shared with regulators and other external stakeholders
- ○ Constant cost competition
- ○ Pressure to customize products to niches and even individual consumers
- ○ Just-in-time product delivery
- ○ Information explosion and specialization
- ○ Employee expectations of participation in decisions

Management's response to these pressures has been to move to an organizational style that has variously been described as "networked," "clustered," "nonhierarchical," "horizontal," or simply "flatter." Some of the characteristics of such organizations are:

- ○ Reliance on temporary, cross-organizational teams
- ○ Decision-making authority distributed to operational personnel
- ○ Flattening of the management hierarchy—removal of layers of approvals
- ○ Providing an open information environment
- ○ Teaming with suppliers
- ○ Teaming with customers
- ○ Alliances with other organizations, even competitors
- ○ Continuous emphasis on quality improvement
- ○ Constant education and training
- ○ Making customer service and sales everyone's business

These management trends will have important implications for not only the frequency of these meetings but the kinds of meetings that will occur in the future. We believe these trends will result in:

- ○ *Significant increase in the number of meetings.* Virtually all of the management trends listed above will result in an increase in both the number and scope of meetings. The number of required meetings increases (1) when people in your organization work in teams, (2) when your company's decisions are made horizontally rather than vertically, and (3) when your customers and suppliers are included in the decisions. Including more people in decisions may have tremendous payoffs during implementation, but if you are a wise manager, you will soon realize that reaching a decision with more involvement almost always means more meetings.

○ *Increase in physical distance.* Expect costs to escalate if everybody has to be physically present at a meeting. When more people—whether from the same organization, from different parts of the organization, or from other organizations—are included in the decision-making process, the costs will soar. Not only is there the cost associated with travel and lodging, but there is also the cost of the salaries of all the meeting participants while they are attending the meetings. By taking key people physically away from their tasks frequently, a firm may be putting itself in jeopardy by not having proper leadership immediately available during a time of crisis.

○ *Pressure to provide access to all information.* If you are going to have "empowered" teams making decisions, you had better recognize that these teams need direct and open access to information. A major barrier to reaching agreement among the different units of an organization can occur when each unit comes to the discussion with different information about the same issue.

Ordinarily, the hierarchy plays an integrating function, with managers obtaining the information they need from their organizational counterparts so they can pass it on to their subordinates. But in highly decentralized organizations, with fewer managers and more reliance on teams, this job of integrating information from throughout the organization and distributing it to others will not be served by the management hierarchy. Also, as the number of meetings increases (with corresponding increases in travel time and costs), there will be strong management pressure to reduce the number of meetings that are held just to provide information. Management will turn, instead, to electronic communication as a means of keeping people informed and ensuring integration.

○ *Shift in meeting focus—collaboration, not briefing.* Many meetings focus on briefing everyone present about plans that require implementation. At such meetings, people are given goals and assigned tasks, and the work itself is performed later, outside the meeting environment. In the future, however, meetings will stress collaboration rather than briefings. Pressures to address immediately such issues as reducing product delivery time and responding to customer concerns will require that work actually be performed at the meetings themselves and by the entire team.

To make this work, meetings must permit intense interaction among participants. A precondition for this is to allow everyone access to the same information. Tasks that are done better by individuals must still somehow be incorporated into the work being done by the team.

○ *Consensual decision making.* Decisions need to be reached in a timely manner. But many of the temporary teams of the future will need to work largely by consensus, or mutual agreement. If product schedules or customer demands are to be met, teams made up of representatives of multiple organizations cannot continually go back to their managers to resolve conflicts between the organizations but must resolve those crises immediately.

The team members must work together, with all having access to the same information. Yet the ease or difficulty with which people work together in meetings will depend upon the creation of cooperative relationships and require a supportive, encouraging atmosphere. These are significant preconditions for consensual decision making.

○ *Long-term, intense interaction.* In most organizations, the meetings related to any one project occur periodically, with several days or weeks separating them. But when temporary teams work together on crash projects, there must be intense interaction on almost a moment-by-moment basis, for periods of weeks or even months. Temporary teams can be housed together physically for the duration of the project. The alternative is to link them electronically in a way that permits much the same interaction and informal discussion that occur when people are in proximity.

Even more than in the past, in the future meetings will be the glue that binds the organization or the project together. This trend is already visible in young, fast-moving technology companies. Traditional management controls such as budgets and management approvals can no longer serve the same function when the team involved is a temporary one that cuts across functions, includes people from other organizations, and is empowered to make decisions. Instead, the meetings themselves play the control function.

In the absence of well-defined patterns of interaction and control, issues are negotiated in numerous meetings, many quite informal and spontaneous. But when meetings serve as a primary decision point and control mechanism, then senior management needs to ensure the effectiveness of those meetings.

Those future organizations that continue to use the time-honored but also time-worn meetings of today will lose out. They will find themselves at the back of a pack led by organizations that use the technology of the future to work together collaboratively and effectively.

Guideposts for Effective Implementation

Over the next decade organizations will spend billions connecting their employees through technology that will permit collaboration and electronic participation in meetings. Many organizations will find new ways of working together that give them a competitive edge in every aspect of their operations. But hundreds of millions of those dollars will be wasted chasing fads and installing technology that people use to work the same way they worked before they were electronically connected.

In many ways we are all exploring uncharted terrain. It may be a brave new world, but it is also an unknown world, with unknown dangers lurking. It's presumptuous, at this time, for anyone to say he or she can guarantee the proper path to the promised land of effective and efficient organizational collaboration.

But in the meantime, the authors have scanned the horizon for at least a few fixed reference points upon which people can depend, some "guideposts" for people beginning their own explorations. Based upon our interviews of people currently involved in introducing the new technologies, our reviews of the scattered literature, and most of all, our more than 50 years as organizational change agents (external and internal), our counsel is as follows:

1. *Treat introduction of collaborative technologies as a major management issue, not a technology issue.* Everything we have seen so far, in our own experience and the experience of others, shows that most people use new technologies to work the way they always have, just faster or easier. If this happens with the new collaboration technologies, most of their value will be lost. The value of the new technologies will be realized only when people invent entirely new ways of collaborating. The failure to realize the potential of the new collaborative technologies is most likely to occur if the focus is on the technology, not the collaboration. The focus on how people within an organization collaborate makes it a management issue, not just something that belongs in the Information Technology group. Implementing significant use of the new technologies requires people organization-wide to change how they work together. That change may be for the better, but it's still change, and it will elicit the usual resistance to change. There are bound to be winners and losers. There will be a redistribution of turf. There is great risk in making the kind of investment the new technology will require if you do not engage management in planning the implementation of a significant program of organizational change.

2. *Target the improvement of meeting effectiveness (and all the ways people collaborate in your organization) as a major opportunity*

to improve organizational productivity. Most companies have no conscious program to improve meeting effectiveness specifically or collaboration generally. Without adequate preparation, people must acquire the skills of meeting leadership and meeting participation—and there are specific skills involved for both roles—by osmosis, if at all. Companies that invest hundreds of millions of dollars to have the most competitive manufacturing processes in the world may have antiquated and wasteful meeting processes. What is the point of investing millions in collaborative technology if you are not spending any time thinking about how people work together in meetings now, with or without technology?

3. *Look at the total "collaboration system," not just the technology.* There is a considerable danger that the new technology will prevail without its users' understanding the equally significant changes that have occurred in our knowledge of how to stimulate creativity, encourage resolution of disputes, visualize complex processes, and design physical spaces that support interaction. Collaboration technology will not have much payoff if different parts of the organization do not share information, if crucial stakeholders are excluded from the problem solving, or if collaboration is a threat to the functional chain of command. Management should be worried about a limited return on investment if excellent technology is put in the service of a limited understanding of what meetings are or could be.

During the preparation of this book the authors came across technologists who were clearly at the cutting edge of technology but had virtually no knowledge of the "group process" field, nor showed any interest in it. We watched a few so-called "meetings of the future" where the technology was highly advanced but served a concept of what a meeting could be that had most of the same characteristics of a meeting between a feudal monarch and his knights. We also saw group process specialists recoil in horror at the idea of using the new technologies, labeling them "dehumanizing." A few important concerns were raised, but many simply expressed a visceral repulsion to anything technological.

The organizations that will truly benefit from collaboration technologies are organizations that look for the synergies among meeting technologies, meeting process, and meeting facilities, and do it all in the larger context of the culture of the organization. The technologists will discover the group process people, the facilities people, and the human resources people (or whoever in the organization is responsible for issues of corporate culture and organizational development), and they will work together as a team. Unless this occurs, there is even some danger that the technology could constrain rather than support continued exploration of how human beings can work together productively.

The essence of what we are saying is to think about human relationships first, then think about how technology can support them. As you will be seeing in later chapters, the human relationships can clearly dominate how the technology is used. Technology in a given organization may never be employed because two parts of the organization are mad at each other! The technology may be wonderful, but it will not work if the organization does not value collaboration enough to manage it effectively.

3

The Collaboration System of the Organization

Bill Gates, the remarkably successful founder and CEO of Microsoft, only meets with other members of his senior management team about once a month. His two principal tools of management are: (1) sending about 100 e-mail messages a day, and (2) spending approximately 70% of his time in small review meetings with product development teams.

Put simply, more than 70% of Bill Gates's time (and that of most senior managers) is spent in some sort of meeting, either formal or informal—and the rest of the time is spent communicating some other way. The bottom line is that management is about creating linkages and direction among the disparate parts of the organization. Management is about ensuring collaboration.

Meetings are as central to the effectiveness of the organization as budgets are to the organization's financial control system and recording keeping is to its accounting system. Meetings play a crucial role in communication and control, particularly nonhierarchical control, in the modern organization.

This view is particularly well stated in a report prepared for the 3M Corporation by Lynn Oppenheim of the Wharton Center, who describes meetings as one of three control systems in the organization. The first control system is the hierarchical structure of the organization itself, the classic delineation of lines of authority. The second is the financial control system of budgets, cost centers, auditing, and other mechanisms that provide information to the organization about how it is using its financial resources. The third, she argues, is meetings, or, as she puts it, "meeting systems." In her report "Making Meetings Matter," she states:

> How do meetings control the managerial workflow? They exert their control over the decision processes of an organization, the central work of managers. It is the meeting system which focuses the time and attention of managers. Holding meetings targets these key resources on some issues or problems at the expense of others. Decisions made at the meeting further affect asset resource allocation. Meetings are one of the places where organizational trade-offs are played out. . . .
>
> The decision process and the meeting system are quite closely linked. Very often, a decision in an organization is not an isolated act at one point in time by an individual, but the result of efforts of many people over an extended period of time. The integration of these efforts is one of the primary roles played by the meeting system. . . .
>
> Meetings provide a uniquely flexible control system. It is integrative and immediate, particularly effective in situations of change. We hypothesized that meetings would be used more often in "younger" companies, where the issues were more likely to be uncertain or unclear and the authority patterns less firmly established. And indeed, the difference between the amount of time spent in meetings between older and younger companies in our sample is significant.[1]

What Do We Know About Meetings?

Ironically, for all the time corporate America spends in meetings, there is not a great deal of hard information about meetings. In 1989 the 3M Corporation sponsored a study on meetings conducted by the Annenberg School of Communication.[2] This study provides a unique baseline of meeting life before the introduction of many of the technologies that will form the basis for cybermeetings.

Annenberg researchers interviewed 903 people from 36 small, medium, and large organizations in the public and private sectors. Participants included Honeywell, Great Western Bank, the Automobile Club of Southern California, Hughes Aircraft, Pacific Bell, Southern California Edison, the Minnesota Department of Education, and the United Way of Los Angeles. The results provide the profile of a typical meeting in America in 1989.

Such a meeting can be described as:

○ More likely to be a staff meeting than any other type (45% of all meetings reported)
○ Taking place in a company conference room (74%)
○ Lasting an hour and 30 minutes
○ Attended by nine people (two managers, four coworkers, two subordinates, and one outsider)
○ Having two hours' notification that the meeting would take place
○ Having no written agenda distributed in advance (63%)
○ Being somewhat or very informal (76%)
○ Involving active participation from most or all attendees (72%)
○ Utilizing handouts (47%)
○ Covering the agenda completely only half the time (53%)
○ Having 11% of the time spent talking about irrelevant issues

In addition to staff meetings—quite possibly the most reviled kind of meeting—the other most frequent types of meetings were task force meetings (22%) and information sharing meetings (21%). See Figure 1.

Figure 1. Pie chart showing frequency of various types of meetings.

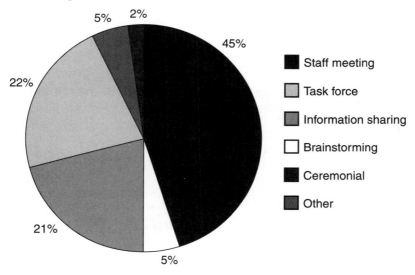

The most frequent purposes for meetings were to:

○ Communicate information.	29%
○ Reach a group judgment or decision.	26
○ Solve a problem.	11
○ Ensure that everyone understands.	11
○ Facilitate staff communication.	5
○ Gain support for a program.	4
○ Explore new ideas and concepts.	4
○ Reconcile conflicting views.	3
○ Accept reports.	2
○ Demonstrate a project or system.	2
○ Relieve tension by providing information.	1

So, what do people talk about in those meetings?

Operational Topics

○ Organizational update	16%
○ Workload and project management	14

○ Product or service issues   14
○ Miscellaneous operational issues   8
○ Policies and procedures   6
○ Human resource management   5
○ Financial issues   4

Strategic Topics

○ Organizational development   10%
○ Improving productivity   8
○ Strategic goal setting   6
○ Product and service planning   4
○ Marketing   3

Other Significant Findings

○ 61% of all meetings are attended by 15 people or fewer.
○ In a third of all meetings, only a few or some of the relevant people attended the meeting.
○ People in large organizations attend significantly more meetings.

So what does this tell us? Just for a start, the most common type of meeting is also the most frustrating. Research and practical experience show that most people hate staff meetings *and* most people feel they are essential. They are often seen as the least efficient meetings, plagued with politics and the need to massage the boss's ego, and encumbered by the need of key lieutenants to make points with the boss. But nobody seems to know how to do without them. Everybody seems to know that large amounts of time are wasted, yet something seems to be taking place during that time that people want and need if they are going to identify with the team. But obviously if a blend of the new group and electronic technologies can make a difference, staff meetings are a good place to start. But they are going to have to be sure to address this hidden dimension that keeps bringing people back even when the meeting is too long, badly organized, and frequently off the track.

The other thing that emerges from the Annenberg research is that meetings do not seem to receive much planning.

In their sample of meetings, 33% of the participants had spent no time preparing for the meeting, and 44% had spent 1 to 60 minutes. (On the other hand, if participants only knew about the meeting 2 hours ahead, it's unlikely that much work has gone into structuring this meeting to make it as effective as possible.)

Every manual on effective meetings advises careful planning in advance of the meeting. That is not going to occur if most meetings happen on the spur of the moment. People will fall back on standard organizational expectations of what meetings look like. If the meeting of the future is really going to be different, people must be able to use the new meeting tools without days of preparation and planning (although that may be entirely justified for major team or product meetings).

This means that the advance thinking has to take place at the system or culture level. New expectations and skills for meetings have to be sufficiently instilled so that they can be called upon without much need for preparation. Organizations need to take responsibility for how efficient and effective their meeting systems are, not by focusing on individual meetings but by looking at the skills base, attitudes, and procedures that drive meetings organization-wide.

WHY MEETINGS FAIL

Participants in the Annenberg study report that the most frequent causes of unsuccessful meetings are:

- Lack of notification—lack of preparation time
- No agenda
- Wrong people in attendance
- Lack of control or influence in meetings
- Political pressure
- Hidden agenda

Meeting Systems

The Annenberg study also reported that meetings do not occur in isolation; they are surrounded by other work and other forms of collaboration. Fully 24% of the study participants reported they had already attended five or more meetings on the same topic, and the same percentage expected to attend five or more additional meetings on the topic. Only 17% reported no prior meetings on the same topic, and only 19% expected no additional meetings. This includes only those interactions that people identified as meetings. It does not include conversations in the hall or coffee room, phone conversations, or videoconferences.

The reality of life in an organization is that topics are not resolved in a single meeting. There is a continuing dialogue about these topics, in a number of forums. Lynn Oppenheim of the Wharton Center says that if meetings are going to be effective our focus needs to be shifted from the meeting to the "meeting system":

> Meetings are rarely single events. At the very least they are embedded in a cycle of preparation and follow-up. . . . More often, individual meeting cycles are connected over time in "meeting systems," a series of meetings on a particular problem or issue. The series may have sub-meetings to deal with discrete tasks, such as committees of a board of directors. These meetings are all connected and extend over time, hence we label them a "meeting system." If we view meetings as a system, rather than as a single event with a single set of outcomes, it becomes clear that meetings occur in a context. Events that occur outside the meeting room can have as much effect on the meeting as events that occur within.[3]

Ray Grenier and George Metes, in their book *Going Virtual*, present a similar view:

> Think of a project as a carefully designed continuous meeting, a process by which collaborative work is

accomplished primarily through electronic communications. The conducting medium changes according to need: face-to-face, audio conference, video conference, computer conferencing, and so forth. But only the medium changes; the medium is always there, holding the virtual team together in a value producing network. Meetings are no longer events for reviewing the past, casting blame, and wasting everyone's time, but rather the conceptual basis of the work process.[4]

Not only do "meeting systems" last over time, but the requirements change for what kind of interaction is required. There may be periods of intense interaction followed by periods where individuals work alone, followed by another period of interaction.

The Collaboration System

The American Heritage Dictionary defines a *meeting* as "the act or process of coming together; encounter." In this broad sense, there will always be meetings. But "coming together, encounter" occurs in many ways. Thinking of meetings as a system, not an event, is an extremely important insight, but the insight needs to be extended to thinking of meetings as part of an organization's **collaboration system.**

Jim Creighton, one of the authors, was recently on the phone with a manager from a major high-tech company that is seriously pursuing the market for desktop-based videoconferencing. When Jim mentioned that he was working on a book about cybermeetings, this manager rather sternly informed him that his company does not have any products related to meetings, but is interested only in the "collaborative work environment." Another consultant friend, part of a team that designs and builds interactive meeting spaces, informed us that he discourages meetings and instead proposes highly interactive workshops coupled with extensive electronic communication.

Both are trying to get at an important point: Meetings are the visible symbol of a much larger system of collaboration. Meetings are the workhorse of an organization's collaboration system. But the kind of communication that occurs between two or more people mediated by their computers (the "desktop environment") is as much a part of the collaboration system as the annual budget review held in the boardroom.

Think of all the purposes the collaboration system serves:

○ Information is given. (This is most effective when the information is given in an interactive manner, with an opportunity for questions or discussion.)
○ Relationships are built.
○ Decisions are made.
○ Resources and time are allocated.
○ Disputes are resolved.
○ Commitment to decisions or direction is built.
○ Ideas are generated.
○ Planning is done.
○ Successes are celebrated.

To accomplish all these purposes, the collaboration system includes a variety of formal, highly structured events and casual, informal events, as shown in Figure 2.

A technology or process that may be very supportive of one meeting purpose may get in the way if used in another type of meeting. A formal meeting may require an extensive array of technology and group process tools, while an informal conversation in the cafeteria might best be supported by some form of on-line access in the cafeteria, possibly using a **personal digital assistant** (a palm-size computer with cellular phone access to the intranet). This does not mean that technology is less useful for less formal meetings; technology may have its greatest power linking up informal discussions to the broader collaborative process. Technology would, for example, permit team members to broadcast ideas generated in an informal discussion to other team members. Later in the afternoon they might already be discussing drawings or figures via desktop videoconferencing. By the next day they might

Figure 2. How people collaborate.

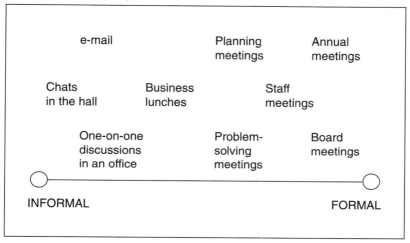

have a plan or prototype that would justify a more formal project meeting. The technology would change with each kind of interaction, but its purpose remains the same: providing the linkages that make it easy for people to collaborate.

It's also clear that improving the collaboration system will require making changes in far more than technology. It will also require changes in meeting process, such as using structured processes to stimulate creativity or expedite decision making. It will also require changes in meeting facilities, such as the hypothetical FutureTech interactive meeting center in Chapter One. These changes will interact within a broader context, the culture of the particular organization in which they are being applied. (See Figure 3.) Different organizations have different norms and practices related to collaboration, dispute resolution, teaming, and formality. Ingredients that are enthusiastically embraced in one culture may be rejected in others.

Our discussion turns now to changes that will be needed in each of these components to optimize the impact the new technologies will have on the collaboration system. We start with the broader picture, the organizational climate in which these changes are taking place.

Figure 3. Components of the collaboration system.

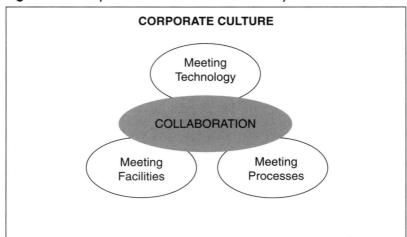

Notes

1. Lynn Oppenheim, "Making Meetings Matter: A Report to the 3M Corporation," Wharton Center for Applied Research, Inc., Philadelphia, Penn., December 1987, p. 13. Reprinted by permission of 3M Visual Systems Division, Austin, Texas.
2. Peter R. Monge, Charles McSween, and JoAnne Wyer, Annenberg School of Communications, University of Southern California, November 1989.
3. Oppenheim, op. cit., p. 11.
4. Ray Grenier and George Metes, *Going Virtual* (Upper Saddle River, N.J.: Prentice-Hall, 1995), p. 58.

4

Collaborative Technology and Corporate Culture

An acquaintance of ours once described the impact of corporate culture this way: "In my old organization I got sent off to management training courses where I heard about all kinds of innovations, some of which I found very intriguing. But within the first week after my return the organization successfully inoculated me against the danger that I would actually use any of these innovations. It was clear that having fulfilled its obligation to send me to training, the company expected me to express my gratitude by not rocking the boat. It was only when I came to my new company and people not only failed to suppress new ideas but actually got excited about them that I began to seriously consider using anything I'd learned during all that training."

Corporate cultures can indeed act like an immune system, with fellow employees patrolling the corridors ready to pounce like killer T cells upon any innovation. Corporate cultures can also sustain and nurture innovations, creating an environment where employees are not only expected to seek out innovation but are actively rewarded for it. The harsh reality is that the meeting innovations described in this book simply will not have much payoff in some organizations, because the culture of those organizations does not support the values that are needed to encourage their effective use. There are preconditions in corporate culture that are needed if these innovations are to flourish and grow.

Corporate Culture Preconditions

The examples of cybermeetings depicted in Chapter One either explicitly mentioned or implied that these corporate culture conditions prevailed at FutureTech:

- ○ Emphasis on horizontal problem solving rather than hierarchical decision making
- ○ Open access to information for employees
- ○ Reliance on temporary, cross-organizational teams
- ○ Inclusion of major suppliers and/or customers in designing products or planning to provide services—"partnering"

Emphasis on Horizontal Problem Solving

At Madison Square Garden (MSG), where Jim Adams is busy helping that company roll out many of the innovations described in this book, there are 500 events a year, including 44 New York Knicks (NBA) games (not counting playoff games), 90 Christmas Carol performances, 44 New York Rangers (NHL) games, 30 concerts, and 20 family shows. As can be imagined, it takes a small army of well-organized people to ensure that each event goes on as flawlessly as possible.

Planning for these events typically requires the involvement of all MSG organizational elements as well as outside promoters, officials, support staff, and press. Time pressure alone means that decisions have to be made horizontally. There is no time to buck decisions to management. There cannot be people so bent out of shape that they cannot work together tomorrow to manage another major event.

It's this need for horizontal collaboration that's driving Madison Square Garden to use cybertechnologies. Yet compared to most major companies, MSG is highly compact. All of those people work within one large city block primarily in two large buildings (although it can still take 15 minutes to get from one building to the next). Some employees make this round trip four to eight times a day. That's 1 to 2 hours of productive time lost daily just walking back and forth between buildings.

Imagine what happens in organizations facing the same kind of time pressures to get products to market, or services to customers, with the key staff sprawled across the globe! Many of these organizations are moving to flatter organizations, with less hierarchy and more decision-making authority at the operational level. Increasingly CEOs see their role as instilling the strategic vision rather than making the day-to-day decisions.

But in a number of organizations, particularly in older, more traditional areas of business and government, decision making remains largely hierarchical. We frankly question the value that the new technologies will bring to such organizations. The value of making it possible for anybody in the organization to participate anytime, anyplace* is dramatically reduced if employees are required to stay within their organizational stovepipes and are not going to influence the decision anyway. It only has value in a corporate culture where participation is valued and could make a difference.

Open Access to Information

The basic thrust of the new technologies is toward increased employee access to information. In our FutureTech examples in Chapter One, Roseann's team is able to resolve a major argument over marketing strategies by accessing a database from the meeting room, with the information projected on the wall, for all to see. When even that will not resolve one issue, they broadcast a request for further information to a researcher outside the room, and a few minutes later get their answer, once again for all to see. Similarly, Bob and Gail, working in

---

* In Silicon Valley, "anytime, anyplace" is a kind of mantra that is repeated as a goal of most collaborative work products. The phrase can be attributed to Stanley M. Davis, *Future Perfect* (Reading, Mass.: Addison-Wesley, 1987).

a coffee lounge, come up with a whole new technical approach because when they need the information about an old, apparently unrelated project, they can access it immediately right there in the lounge.

Not all disputes are over facts. But when they are, there is tremendous power in having employees be able to access those facts immediately and in ways that help them address their problems.

One of the most powerful insights of the total quality management movement, and now the open book management,[1] is that when people have the information they need they are motivated to excel and redirect their behavior as needed to get the desired result.

Technology can provide the access to the data, but there is little point if corporate culture erects barriers to using that information, or if control over information is a way of exercising power or protecting status or rank. This is not to suggest there are not real issues of security or protection of trade secrets. But increasingly, organizations are finding that with some judicious exceptions, access to information is one of the most powerful tools an organization can provide its employees.

Cross-Organizational Teams

There is so much talk about teams these days that it's almost embarrassing to list teams as an innovation. But so often the rhetoric of teams exceeds the reality. You cannot make a group of people a team just by putting them in a room and calling them one. High-performance teams are built upon trust and confidence, the members' understanding of each other's strengths (and weaknesses), a deep commitment to a common goal, and an almost fanatical desire to succeed in reaching that goal. This is not accomplished by rhetoric alone.

But despite the excessive rhetoric about teams, the use of cross-organizational teams to design a product or deliver a service is becoming a staple of life in many organizations.

Functional organizational structure is very good at solving some problems, and not good at all at solving others. For organizations operating in fast-moving industries, bringing a new product to market while staying carefully within functional lines is nearly suicidal. A substantial body of research shows that teams drawing effectively on the knowledge and resources of a number of organizational units are far more nimble, and typically more creative, than teams working only within a defined functional area.[2]

Most of the team room technologies and group process innovations in our FutureTech examples (Chapter One) are targeted precisely at sustaining and enhancing the effectiveness of teams. But their effectiveness is constrained unless the corporate culture clearly values teams and will commit the resources to ensure their success.

Partnering With Customers and Suppliers

If you have heard a crashing sound around your building lately it is probably the sound of crashing walls. Organizations have discovered that they simply cannot afford the walls and barriers that divide different parts of the organization. Virtually all information from one part of the organization will be available to all others on the organization's intranet. Processes will be reengineered in such a way that they will begin to blur most functional divisions of authority and power.

Hang on to your hats. The front door just blew in, and the outside walls may not be there long. If trends in Silicon Valley are any indication, and they often are, the product design team of the future will include not just people from within your organization, but major suppliers and major customers as well. All have a shared interest in the success of each new product. They can maximize the benefit for everybody by acting as if they were a true team, even though they work for different organizations.

This is a dramatic shift, and it's not just confined to Silicon Valley. One of Jim Creighton's government clients, a senior official with the Army Corps of Engineers, describes an experience he had early in his career. He was managing a construction contract that was being carried out by a major construction firm. Because the project was at a remote location, both the Corps staff and the contractor staff had set up their headquarters in the same trailer. A wall had been built dividing the trailer in half, with a small sliding door in the wall. When the Corps wanted to issue a change order it would knock on the door and pass through the specifications. A few hours later there would be a knock on the door, and a quote would come back through the other way. Not surprisingly, with this kind of communication, the project was soon over budget and off schedule.

Today, after a contract is issued, the Corps would invite the contractor, and major subcontractors, to engage in a process called "partnering." The process would be kicked off with a team building session during which all the parties begin to build relationships and develop agreements about group objectives, decision making, communication norms, and how disagreements will be handled. This would be summarized in a charter, with more details specified in a partnering implementation plan developed over the next few weeks.

After the initial workshop, many aspects of the projects are co-managed. When decisions cannot be reached by mutual agreement, the agreed-upon plan for resolving disagreements is put into action. The results have been so dramatic for the Corps, and other Department of Defense agencies, that the Department of Defense is implementing the approach on environmental cleanup projects throughout the world, working as partners with environmental regulators, contractors, and even the local community.[3]

The Defense Department is not alone. Hundreds of organizations are finding ways of working with other organizations as informal partners. Not only will this trend continue, it will be greatly aided by the new technologies. Information about a project can be shared via computer, possibly by setting up restricted home pages on either the Internet or on an intranet. Desktop videoconferencing will allow all members of the team to stay in constant contact. E-mail can be used to send materials to every member of the team instantly, anywhere in the world. If appropriate, all members of the team will be housed for short stays at a skunkworks facility but stay linked electronically back to their home organizations.

The Constraining Influence of Corporate Culture

Even those organizations that strongly support use of cyber-technologies may stumble over their own corporate culture. Although many of these technologies are just now being implemented, the early findings from research on the impacts of their introduction show how organizational constraints can limit the value of the new technologies. Two recent studies are particularly instructive:

STRATIQUEST STUDY

STRATIQUEST, a strategy consulting firm in Ben Lomond, California, conducted a major research study on the use of collaborative technology for Silicon Graphics.[4] Silicon Graphics provided full technical support—equipment, software, training, and support—for the use of its technology in three companies: Minnesota Mining & Manufacturing Company (3M), Varian Oncology Systems Division, and a high-technology manufacturing company that preferred to remain unnamed. STRATIQUEST then studied how the technology was used and the benefits from its use.

The participants identified three benefits they hoped to achieve from use of the technology:

1. Reduction in time-to-market for new products
2. Reduced operating costs through savings in travel time and dollars
3. Increased customer satisfaction through reduced field problems and resolution time

After five months STRATIQUEST reported that:

○ The high-tech manufacturer was able to reduce to 1 month the time for a complex assembly redesign that previously took 3 to 4 months.
○ 3M found that its geographically dispersed rapid prototyping team improved in its ability to share expertise and workload. The result was fewer bottlenecks and faster turnaround at the physical prototyping phase.
○ All three sites reported that use of a variety of media types—audio images, video, 3-D models, and text—led to improved communication, with less time needed for clarification and problem resolution. This in turn led to less time spent on rework. Clearer communication resulted in fewer misunderstandings and mistakes.
○ The high-tech manufacturer reported reduction in the amount of travel time to suppliers as part of the assembly redesign.

In conversations with Jan Dekema, the president of STRATIQUEST, a more complex picture emerges. According to Dekema there were significant benefits for some of the participants, but success was not universal.

Technology was secondary as a constraint on use of the technology. That is not to say that there were not technical issues. Meeting participants sometimes became impatient with the slowness of the videoconferencing images (due to bandwidth problems). But they figured out how to work around this. One solution was to turn on the visual equipment for only those parts of the meeting where visual communication was important, turning it off the rest of the time. They also ran into problems because of incompatible platforms and operating systems at the different sites, but they found ways of solving or working around them.

The big problems turned out to be:

○ People in the organizations often didn't know why they should collaborate.
○ There were organizational disincentives for collaborating in situations where rewards were based on individual or functional performance.

○ When there were prior organizational conflicts, people just wouldn't talk to each other.

One of the problems that showed up was unexpected. Several of the participating companies had expressed the desire to work more closely with suppliers during product design. There had been a screening process to select those suppliers with whom they would work more closely. The selected suppliers were being asked to coproduce parts or assemblies rather than produce an already designed part. They were expected to be a part of the design. Obviously they needed access to information about design processes and specifications if they were going to fulfill that role. But when the chips were down, manufacturing engineers, project managers, and executives were simply not comfortable providing access to important information about design processes and design specifications.

Dekema believes that some of this reluctance was based on genuine concern about competitors' getting the information, giving up a competitive advantage. But he believes that much of it had to do with organizational culture and habit. He points out that all the same risks exist every time a key technical person takes a job with another organization, or organizations enter into a joint venture. Organizations learn to manage those risks, but they have not really learned how to manage the risk of sharing information with suppliers. He believes there was intellectual buy-in to the concept, but people in these organizations were used to arm's-length relationships with people outside their own organization and they simply did not have the attitudes or skills to work in a true partnering relationship with them.

Suppliers, on the other hand, consistently complained of the need for more information. They instantly grasped the advantages of collaboration but said that information was essential if they were to do their job. One of the pitfalls for a supplier is to be picked for a special relationship with a manufacturer, in the process giving up relationships with competitors of that manufacturer, and then be unable to fulfill the special relationship because it cannot get the information it needs to fulfill its expected role.

The STRATIQUEST study showed that how people felt about the benefits of collaborative technology depended on where they sat in the organization. Executives were the key drivers for launching this study. They were looking forward to a large-scale impact, expecting savings on the order of $10 million a month or more. It was obvious that savings of this magnitude could not be achieved by reducing travel costs. They could only be achieved by having a major impact upon time to market or by producing cost reductions through working more closely with suppliers. Intuitively, and based on their observations, senior managers believed savings of this size could be achieved through collaboration.

Project managers were worried about immediate project costs, including travel costs. But their real concern was not the cost of the travel itself, but the downtime associated with it. Their biggest problem had to do with bottlenecks and delays due to key technical people being tied up while traveling.

At the level of users, such as CAD designers, cost was not an issue. That simply was not their problem. Their question, first and foremost, was: "Does it fit (support) the way I work?" If the technology required them to change the way they worked, they were not interested. Examples of comments received were: "Engineers don't do that," and "That's not part of my job."

STUDY OF A MAJOR CONSULTING GROUP

Another study reinforces the role that organizational factors play in the success of new technology. Wanda J. Orlikowski of the Center for Information Systems Research at Massachusetts Institute of Technology studied the introduction of the groupware software Lotus Notes into a very large management consulting firm. This consulting firm, which Orlikowski refers to as Alpha Corporation (a pseudonym), purchased and distributed Lotus Notes to all its consultants and support staff. The motivation, as described by a senior principal of the firm, was to "leverage the expertise of the firm." The principals believed that Alpha was not using information technology as effectively as it could relative to its competitors, and was falling short in meeting client expectations.[5]

After tracking the introduction of Notes for 5 months, using unstructured interviews, reviewing office documents, and observing work sessions and training classes, Orlikowski reached two major conclusions:

1. People need to be taught a new "mental model" before groupware will be used in a collaborative manner. When the software was introduced without training people to appreciate the collaborative nature of such software, they used it as they had previous software—as a tool to improve personal productivity, not as a way to collaborate.
2. When the rewards of an organization encourage individual performance rather than collaboration, groupware on its own won't engender collaboration.[6]

In particular, Alpha's reward system inhibited the collaborative use of Notes. Like most consulting firms, there is tremendous interest at Alpha in the percentage of time that each consultant works for a client—"billable hours." Using Notes was not seen as a client-related activity and therefore was not chargeable. So people were not willing to spend much time experimenting with its use, or to give up personal time to learn it or use it. While people would use Notes for e-mail or as a database—uses that amounted to only a few minutes a day—they saw more extensive use as disrupting the balance between billable time and personal time, and therefore to be avoided.

Also, within Alpha there are relatively few promotions to "principal" (the highest position in the firm). Competition is fierce, and described by the consultants themselves as cutthroat. Consultants want to develop an area of expertise that makes them stand out, as individuals. They try to maximize opportunities for themselves. Sharing information runs counter to this competitive environment, especially when it's at odds with self-interest.

Interestingly, the firm's technologists, who are not as subject to the competitive culture, are using Notes to work jointly to solve technical problems. Also, the principals of the firm, now above the competitive fray, work far more collaboratively than the consultants, who are still striving to be principals.

In both studies the major barriers to implementation proved to have far more to do with corporate culture and old ways of doing things than with technical problems. Only meeting technologies were introduced. There was no attention to the other ingredients of cybermeetings, such as corporate culture, or meeting processes, or facilities. We believe the results of these studies demonstrate the value of an integrated approach that simultaneously addresses both the technology and organizational issues.

Summing Up

Corporate culture provides a context in which innovations may either flourish or wither and die. Introducing new technologies without simultaneously looking at corporate culture increases the likelihood that your organization will not receive the full benefits of its investment. Nobody can completely predict how corporate culture and the new collaborative technologies will interact, but these principles clearly apply:

- ○ When the rewards in an organization favor individual performance, people are unlikely to engage in collaborative behavior.
- ○ When there are organizational conflicts, people will not use collaborative technology to work with those they see as opponents or adversaries.
- ○ People tend to view a new technology in light of previous technologies and, without some intervention, will use the new technology to work the same old way.

Notes

1. John Case, *Open Book Management* (New York: HarperBusiness, 1995).
2. See Steven Goldman et al., *Agile Competitors and Virtual Organizations* (New York: Van Nostrand Reinhold, 1995), and Richard Tanner Pascale, *Managing on the Edge* (New York: Simon & Schuster, 1990).
3. "Partnering Guide for Environmental Missions of the Air Force, Army, Navy," July 1996. Available from the U.S. Army Corps Institute for Water Resources, Fort Belvoir, Va. Jim Creighton of Creighton & Creighton, and Jerome Delli Priscoli of the Institute were principal authors, under the direction of a Tri-Service Committee.
4. STRATIQUEST, "The Benefits of Collaborative Computing: An Independent Multi-Company Study," 1996. Available from Stratiquest, 353 Rancho Rio Road, Ben Lomand, Calif. 95005-9477.
5. Wanda J. Orlikowski, "Learning from Notes: Organizational Issues in Groupware Implementation," Center for Information Systems Research, Sloan School of Management, MIT, CISR WO No. 241, May 1992.
6. Ibid.

5

Meeting Technology

The first decade of PCs was about putting the power of the computer on everybody's desk. But the machines could not talk to each other. Tremendously valuable information might be stored in your computer, but your coworkers could not access it unless you put it on a disk and handed or mailed it to them. Also, because it was in your machine, they might not even know you had it. This was like a library with no card file or central directory. Each computer was a separate book with its own table of contents that you could access only if you had the right password. It did not matter that you had the information, because nobody knew which book it was in.

By the end of the first decade of the PC, there were modems that would allow you to transmit—slowly and painfully—the information electronically. But anyone who ever tried to transmit things over anything but a dedicated modem line soon found that the bigger problem was to get the machines to have the proper settings to talk the same language. Transmitting the file took only 10 minutes, but that was after 45 minutes on the phone trying to get the two machines to talk to each other.

This experience even inspired one science-fiction writer to write a satire about a society in which each car manufacturer designed its cars so they could be driven only on highways that met their standards. So there were Chrysler highways, Ford highways, GM highways, Toyota highways, and so on. The society was ready to collapse because of the burden of constructing and providing space for this multitude of highways. Of course this was a thinly veiled poke at computer manufacturers that tried to lock users into their proprietary standards at the expense of the larger society.

The second decade of PCs is about "total connectivity," that is, making it easy for the machines to talk with each other and making it easy to find out where all those valuable information resources are located. Within organizations all those computers are being hooked up to networks. A new breed of computer and software "servers" has been designed to talk with all the other computers and do the translation so that the computer on your desk can talk its own language, the computer on someone else's desk can talk its own language, and yet you can pass information back and forth without even being aware it's being translated—at least, that is the dream. The next step is to hook up all the computers in your organization through intranets, and then hook up your server to all the other servers around the world on the Internet.

The goal is to make the communication among all the machines "seamless." That is, except for information protected by codes and "firewalls" to protect trade secrets and other proprietary information, you will not really need to distinguish among what is in your machine, what is inside the organization's network, and what is on the Internet. The state-of-the-art software is being designed so you will not actually be aware of when you have been switched from the internal network to the international network. It's also being designed to "push" information to you; that is, you preselect the topics of interest and it scans the intranet and Internet constantly and, when it finds something on a topic in which you are interested, sends that information to you by e-mail.

Still another trend is to communicate with more and more senses. Anybody who has tried to describe a picture over the telephone knows how much easier it is to talk about it if both people have the same picture in front of them. What would happen if both people could not only see the same picture but could make corrections at each end that could be viewed by the person at the other? They could talk about the proposed changes, erase those changes and try some others, and finally have a revised design that they could both send off to their bosses, who would get the new design electronically within seconds. If you can send words and pictures, why not send 3-D or even holographic models? And rather than sending fixed, static images, how about sending simulations of whole processes, so you can actually see what happens from beginning to end?

The goal is to make the transition seamless among all these media. Working from a single familiar desktop (the image you see when you first turn on your computer), people will be able to send and receive information in all these different sensory modes without having to consciously turn on additional software or use different commands. They will move from Internet to intranet, from desktop videoconferencing to phone to fax, all without leaving their desks.

Meeting Technology Innovations

All this connectivity allows organizations to bring virtually all information resources right into the meeting room. It also allows you to bring people into the meeting room who are not actually in the room, "virtually." And when the meeting is over, it allows you to transmit the results of the meeting easily, at the level of detail desired by people outside the room. Most of the new technologies featured in the scenarios in Chapter One are an outgrowth of this drive for connectivity. These technologies are summarized in Table 1, and some are discussed in the following sections.

Groupware

Groupware permits people at separate locations, even spread around the world, to collaborate as a group from the comfort of their own desks. At present, groupware is primarily targeted at the desktop environment, although there are a number of group-decision-analysis products that are aimed at the team room environment.

Although the term *groupware* makes it sound as if it is

Table 1. Technological ingredients of cybermeetings.

Technological Features	Current Status (1997)
Groupware that permits joint editing of a product— computer-supported collaboration	Such groupware is now available commercially, being rapidly adopted, and rapidly improving.
Multimedia presentations/ modeling/simulation	Software now permits integration of all media in presentations. In the near future, virtually all the modeling and simulation techniques now used in major feature films will be available for office workstations.
Immediate access to databases	With the use of both the World Wide Web (external data) and intranet (internal data), real-time access to data from throughout the world is increasingly becoming a reality in early-adopter companies.
Software agents that can carry out assigned tasks such as scheduling meetings or data searches	Some software agents exist, but no major application for PCs is in wide commercial use.
Meeting room videoconferencing with participation of multiple parties at several sites	This is available commercially.
Desktop videoconferencing	This is available commercially, with dramatic improvements in store.

(Continues)

Table 1. (Continued)

Technological Features	Current Status (1997)
Voice and written interface with the computer	Some commercial applications are available, based on the ability of computers to "learn" a particular individual's voice and writing. Significant work is being expended to develop applications that improve the ability of computers to recognize voice and handwriting universally.
Whiteboard technology/PC-linked projection screens	PC-linked whiteboards—working walls linked to laptop computers—are now available in traditional whiteboard format. Some additional development is needed for mounted boards covering an entire wall. PC-linked projection systems are commercially available. No system currently exists that permits you to write on the whiteboard from your computer, although you can project an image onto the whiteboard and do work within that image.
Wall-size PC-linked projection screens/systems	Very large (although not necessarily wall-size) projection systems are now commercially available, with continued improvements in resolution expected.

Technological Features	Current Status (1997)
Thin-film deposits on walls	Use of thin-film deposit technology to permit whiteboard technology to be applied directly to meeting room walls is not currently available. If this technology is ever developed, it will follow fuller commercial use of PC-linked whiteboards.
Modeling/holographic projections	Holographic projection of computer-aided design (CAD) objects and holographic eyeglasses exist in the laboratory.
Remote viewing headgear	This technology exists in the laboratory.
Expert systems	This technology exists in the laboratory.

solely software, most sophisticated groupware requires both software—such as Lotus Notes, the first widely used groupware application—and a server, a computer whose job it is to link together all the various PCs so they can talk to each other.

As an example, a group might use groupware to edit a group report. In the past, one person would prepare a draft. That report would be sent to the next reviewer, who would suggest corrections, followed by another, then another. The review process often took weeks or months. The process could be shortened by having everybody review the document at the same time. But once all the comments were in, someone had to take the notes laboriously from each reviewer's comments and put them into a master. Often the review comments would be contradictory, requiring continued dialogue to re-solve the dispute.

Using groupware, everybody can bring up the same doc-ument on the screen of their individual PC. They can either attach notes to the document or make actual corrections on the document, with changes from each person shown in a different color. In the event there are significant differences, all members of the team can participate in a desktop videocon-ference. On the monitor of their PC they will see the document as well as the faces of other participants. Everybody can see all the proposed changes. The group can discuss which changes have group consensus. As agreed-upon changes are keyed in, everybody will see the changes in the document on their screen. If the group wants to try out different layouts for the report, individual members can format the report on their own screen, so these alternate formats can be seen by everyone else.

Part of the power of groupware is that people can show each other what they mean, in real time, rather than trying to communicate everything orally. Imagine the advantages of being able to send a set of alternate advertisement layouts to a client halfway around the world and be able to make changes in the layouts jointly, all as part of the same conversation. Rather than try to describe a change in a circuit design, imag-ine being able to make the actual changes on the screen, and then watch and discuss a computer-aided simulation of how well the design works.

Groupware will also be used in the meeting room envi-ronment. Groupware will be used to sort out and display com-ments made by participants by (1) using the PC keyboards mounted in the meeting room table, (2) writing on electronic slates at each seat, or (3) talking into individual microphones. Groupware will also be used to display writing or drawings from the whiteboard to individual monitors, then to display corrections made on individual PCs back up on the whiteboard. Groupware will tie in participants in distant loca-tions so that their comments show up on everybody's moni-tors or on the whiteboard.

Multimedia Presentations/Modeling/Simulation

The simplest way to describe the future of computer-based multimedia is to say that anything that you see in a movie today will be practical in the office meeting room tomorrow. Today you can combine words, graphics, photos, movies, sound, even full orchestration, to increase the effectiveness of a presentation. In the immediate future you will be able to insert computer-generated images in the midst of a video and play it onto a screen. You will have the ability to show computer simulations with 3-D, even holographic, models. This will allow you to try out alternate designs, and actually test how they will work, as part of a normal group discussion.

Immediate Access to Databases

How often have you been in a meeting where an important decision had to be postponed because a critical bit of information was not available? It may have taken days or weeks to find a date for the meeting when everybody could be there. Days were spent in advance preparation. But during the course of the meeting it became clear that more information was needed to resolve a crucial issue. So the decision had to be put off until the next time—weeks away—when everybody could get together again. In the meantime the competition was creeping up behind you.

Let's assume the crucial information existed. It just had to be found. Or it existed in one form, e.g., daily customer orders or production figures, but had not yet been analyzed to answer the critical question. Think of the cost savings if that information could be found, even analyzed, while everybody was still in the room, so that a decision could be made and implemented. It might make the difference in maintaining your competitive edge.

The information may already be available somewhere in your organization. But only if you know who has the information, and can track those individuals down, can you get the information. Often it's not information that is stored on the organization's mainframe computer, since it is viewed as important to only one individual or organizational unit. Even if you had access to everybody's PC, someone would have to go through each PC, searching for the right information.

Imagine the increases in productivity if everybody could have access to all the information inside the organization, and could just pick the relevant information from a menu and have the computer track the information down and display it for use. Ironically, the tools that are making this possible were first developed for the exchange of information around the world on the Internet, and only now are being used *inside* organizations, a use usually described as "intranet." The establishment of the worldwide Internet was originally funded by the National Science Foundation (NSF) to link scientists around the world. One of the problems of science is that by the time information is published in journals, following intensive peer review, much time has passed since the work itself was done. Also, not all the information is ever published. Information that does not seem directly relevant to a researcher considering one problem may be the missing piece for a researcher working on another. Some patterns do not emerge unless the number of cases being evaluated is very large. Since cost limits the size of most studies, one of the valuable tools of science is the ability to aggregate and analyze a number of studies, looking for those patterns that emerge with large numbers of cases. Doing this requires access to the data themselves, not just the conclusions reached by the individual researcher. NSF could see that linking scientists via computer and modem was a way to begin to address these opportunities.

People know a good thing when they see it, and after a while, everybody wanted access to all that good information. Their interest was not just limited to scientific research. They also wanted information about markets and about environmental issues, and they just wanted to be able to talk to other people with similar interests. The Internet provided a medium for all these interests. People kept adding new servers for new users, and the Internet grew like Topsy. There are some conventions—established by a committee that actually has no power—that people observe because the system could not work without conventions. But the Internet is utterly nonhier-archical. Nobody "runs" or "owns" the Internet.

Initially, the information you could get across the Internet was limited to "text," a stripped-down word-based language. The problem is that different computers use different operating systems. So there were DOS customers, Wintel customers, OS/2 customers, UNIX customers, Mac OS customers, and many more. There can be major difficulties communicating to people using a different operating system. The computers can all communicate in "text," but at the expense of losing all the formatting and all the graphics.

The tool that opened up the Internet and turned it into a genuine World Wide Web was a programming language called Hypertext Transfer Markup Language (HTML). What HTML did was to give people a way of highlighting the key words in a document to allow a server to recognize the topics being addressed in the document. With HTML, researchers could also help their friends by referring them to other important documents. Using HTML, the researchers encode a document so that every reference to another document or other sources of information is highlighted in another color. Someone reading the document can simply select (by clicking a mouse or hitting "return") a particular highlighted phrase and find themselves reading that other document, obtained from another computer located somewhere else in the world.

The next step was the development of hypermedia. Hypermedia documents contain links not only to words but also to sounds, images, and even movies. The Web was transformed, seemingly overnight, from words to full multimedia.

Soon the Internet was so large, so complex, and, yes, so chaotic, that the problem was *not* getting access to all that wonderful information, but *knowing where* to look for it. The solution was software that would search the entire Web, looking for documents by using the right key words, giving you a list you could choose from within a matter of a few seconds or minutes. The first step in the development of this software was a browser called Mosaic, developed by the National Center for Supercomputing Applications. The first browser was made available in 1993. A browser allows you to communicate with someone else's computer, display material from that computer, search through the computer for the information that interests you, and then download it. Mosaic was followed by NetScape's Navigator and Microsoft's Explorer, both of which possess improved ability to access graphics, and contain numerous additional features. The next stage was the development of *search engines*. While browsers allow you to locate and download material in someone else's computer if you already know the computer's web address, search engines such as WebCrawler or Excite can hunt through every computer connected to the World Wide Web, looking for the material you want. You type in a key word or words, and soon receive lists (sometimes numbering in the thousands) of sources of information you can access with a few clicks on your mouse. Major new companies, such as Yahoo! and Point Cast, have been formed to help you locate information more easily, customized to your preferences, and to make a profit by helping advertisers find you. In fact, the newest software, created by companies such as Marimba, allows you to specify your interests, and then will "push" the information to you, sending you an e-mail whenever it finds something that might be of interest.

The same tools that allow you to browse the World Wide Web at will also allow you to browse through all that information stored within your own organization. Although the World Wide Web gets most of the press, the intranet may be far more significant for most organizations. If organizations are going to downsize, reengineer processes, and empower employees, as a precondition they will need to provide employees with almost total access to the information assets of the organization.

Software Agents

The late distinguished economist Kenneth Boulding said "wisdom is not having more information. It is knowing which information doesn't matter." [1] While the World Wide Web and intranet provide remarkably expanded access to data, the challenge is to make this information useful. Wouldn't it be nice to have an agent that could run around and find information, and even put it into usable form that would permit you to make decisions? If this agent were smart enough, you could even have the agent set up meetings for you, and complete other repetitive or frustrating tasks—all within limits that you set, of course.

Software agents are already in use in large mainframe applications. For example, when you are making a plane reservation a software agent locates the most convenient time, and with your approval actually arranges for a sale of your seat in the mainframe computer of the airline providing your travel.

Various software producers have claimed to produce software to make agents available to users of PCs. Both authors of this book have experimented with PC-based software claiming to be agents and, based on those experiences, have concluded that agent software at the PC level is promising but it's not there yet. It is developing very rapidly. It has the virtue of having the machines do what machines do well and without noticeable psychological stress, leaving people free to do what they do best.

The promise of agent software is that it can make the technology less visible. When you make your plane reservation, you do not care about all the sophisticated technology that makes it possible. You simply want the process completed quickly and efficiently. The less people have to think about what operations their PC must perform to accomplish a task, the more useful their PC will be. Let your agent decide which software application needs to be opened to perform a task. Let your agent connect you to your organization's intranet or the World Wide Web. If you are in a meeting and the participants need research information, let your agent wander around the Web finding the research information you need, and let your agent format the research information it finds in a manner the group can understand and use immediately, while they are still in the meeting. The more invisible the technology becomes, the more value it will have.

The key to the success of agent technology will, once again, not be just in the software, but in the servers, the computers that link other computers. The servers, which once served primarily to control the sequencing of communications between computer and printers (or other peripherals) now act much like agents in linking PCs to PCs, and PCs to mainframes. They are beginning to do such a good job that they are likely to become a major focus of efforts to make sure technology, not people, does the work.

Meeting Room Videoconferencing

Videoconferencing has been billed as the wave of the future for so long that it already feels like part of the past. Nevertheless, it is very much alive and far more likely to fulfill its promise precisely because it will no longer be just a way of being able to see other participants. By adding groupware, intranet, Internet, and whiteboard technology to videoconferencing, it becomes a much more useful tool.

Desktop videoconferencing will reduce the need for a number of meetings where people are physically assembled in a room, but there will still be plenty of meetings as organizations use more project teams and "partner" with their suppliers and customers. When the task goes beyond the exchange of information, or when there are no prior relationships, most people still prefer personal interaction. There is simply more information available about who the other people are and what they are feeling. There is also an opportunity to interact with people outside their official roles, which often provides even more sense of who they are, an essential ingredient in building trust. Groups will continue to need to work in the meeting room environment when there is a need to build trust and relationships between the participants, when there will be extended interaction justifying the expense of attending a meeting, or when there is a relatively large number of participants.

A number of tools have been developed that make meeting room videoconferencing more useful:

○ The viewing screen can be split into segments so that you can view a number of participants at the same time. You are not limited to focusing solely on the speaker. Part of the information we get from being in a meeting is not just the body language of the speaker but also the body language and visual cues about how people are reacting to what is being presented.

○ People are no longer constrained to a single videoconferencing room. Rollabout videoconferencing systems can be wheeled intact from room to room, so that the system can be used anywhere in a building.

○ The screen can be split to show a document on which the team is working collaboratively, along with the faces of the participants in the discussion. Similarly, the split screen can be used to show video or movie clips.

○ You can move the camera around, while sitting at the table with the group, using a tool not too dissimilar to a turbo ball (a kind of mouse that some people use with their personal computer). The camera can zoom in on a single person, focus on a drawing on the wall, then back off and show the whole group once again.

At this time, one limitation of videoconferencing is that when you view a number of people simultaneously on a split screen, their movements appear jerky and awkward. It does not look like a movie or television. If you remember watching old silent movies, they also appeared jerky and awkward. The reason was that they showed fewer frames per second than a modern film. The "smoothing" out of the picture occurs by showing many more frames, that is, by providing much more information. The same problem still holds true for many videoconferencing systems.

The reason is that you can only cram so much information through a wire. Compare the size of one of your graphics files with a simple word processing file. Graphics eat up your computer memory, because there is so much more information provided with graphics. Imagine the amount of information that has to be transmitted to simultaneously hold a conversation among 4, 8, or even 16 people. You simply cannot stuff all that information through an ordinary phone line.

If everybody in a videoconference is part of the same computer network, videoconferencing occurs at approximately 30 frames, about the same speed as commercial television. As of this writing, a phone-cable–based system using ISDN phone service (a more expensive but increasingly available level of service) achieves a maximum of approximately 24 frames a second. Using ordinary phone lines, it drops to 15 frames per second because of constraints on the amount of information that can be put through the wire. The difference in smoothness is noticeable.

The technical term for the amount of information that can be shoved through a telephone wire in a given period of time is *bandwidth*. For videoconferencing to seem normal, more bandwidth is needed. Videoconferencing is not the only use constrained by bandwidth, and around the world, companies are scurrying to install optic fiber cables to replace conventional telephone cable. More bandwidth can also be created using existing phone cables and a system called asymmetrical digital subscriber line (ADSL) technology, which can vary the amount of traffic in both directions.

The alternative to optic cables is an option being touted by former cellular phone magnate Craig McCaw, who has set up a company to put a ring of satellites around the earth. In this scheme, information will not flow through cables, but will be replaced by satellite transmissions. Cable may still be needed from the satellite antenna to the PCs on people's desks, although even that is not certain. The FCC has recently approved experimental permits for low-power broadcasting systems that could permit wireless communication between computers within a building.

Desktop Videoconferencing

Desktop videoconferencing is readily available commercially. Almost every heavy hitter in the computer industry is rushing to develop new equipment and software to carve out its share of what it expects to be a major market.

One of the attractive prospects of desktop videoconferencing is that the systems simply add on to equipment that's already on most people's desks. The key elements are a minia-ture camera (about the size of a microphone) that mounts right on the monitor facing the meeting participant, a video board that installs in the computer, and software.

Prices can run as low as $1,500 to $2,000 per workstation and will probably get cheaper as the market expands.

Desktop videoconferencing lends itself to quickly called, informal meetings (companies encouraging the development of this technology like to talk about "collaboration" instead of "meetings"). A quick phone conversation can turn into a videoconference that can resolve in minutes an issue that might otherwise require days or weeks of formal meetings. Furthermore, people do not have to spend time going to a meeting room somewhere in the same or a nearby building.

Desktop videoconferencing is constrained even more than meeting room videoconferencing by the limitations posed by bandwidth. When run over a conventional phone line, a desktop system will provide approximately 5 frames per second, compared with 30 frames per second for conven-tional television. This difference is very noticeable. With the amount of money and energy being poured into desktop videoconferencing by major companies, improvements will be coming very rapidly.

Voice and Written Interface With the Computer

Within a very few years, you will have a choice as to whether you communicate with your computer by using your voice, by drawing pictures, by writing things out in longhand, or by using a keyboard. This will begin to make computers genu-inely friendly. Words themselves are an impediment for some people who are very visually oriented. Many people view hav-ing to type words into a keyboard as forcing them to adapt themselves to the computer, rather than the other way around (they are right). Others find their creativity flows only in a relaxed setting where they can just talk things through. They feel blocked in the structured, linear world of the written word. Providing people with options will let them use the mode that's most comfortable for them, and that they find most productive.

Ironically, the group most likely to notice the difference is top management. Many in top management are still uncomfortable using PCs. J. R. Simplot, the Idaho potato king who became the major shareholder in computer manufacturer Micron Technology, has reportedly never used a PC. He is symbolic of a generation of managers who had information management people to run their mainframes. Using keyboards was a clerical function, and having a keyboard in your office diminished your status. This may be a generational thing: The advent of e-mail has made keyboards an essential part of every manager's life, and in the process made top managers less computer-phobic.

In meetings, where most of the interaction is verbal, voice communication with the computer will open up many opportunities. The computer could be instructed to keep a verbatim summary of the meeting or capture verbal summaries of agreements that have been reached. When combined with whiteboard technology, these summaries could be projected onto a wall or a screen, where everybody in the room could view them and verify that the summary was correct. Verbal commands could also instruct the computer to bring up a particular database and project the results, or search for and display a video showing a manufacturing process or alternative design. A holographic image projected into the middle of the room could be ordered to alter size or shape, or change design characteristics in response to verbal commands.

Whiteboard Technology/PC-Linked Projection Screens

It's hard to remember that into the 1960s, the most sophisticated technology in most meeting rooms was a blackboard. Eventually, along came the whiteboard. But there were two fundamental problems with either: (1) When you ran out of space, something had to be erased, so it was lost from group view; and (2) when the meeting was over, someone had to go into the room and recopy everything down on paper. We can remember meetings where the trick was to take a Polaroid shot of the blackboard/whiteboard at the end of the meeting so that everything on the board would not be lost as the next group poured into the meeting room.

The next technology was the flip chart. Ideas could be written on the flip chart pad and posted on the wall. Everything was saved, and as the next group arrived at the meeting room all you had to do was roll up your flip chart sheets. But then somebody had to type everything up laboriously, redrawing any graphics.

There is something about the size of flip chart pads that seems constraining. Big ideas and big projects called out for something on a grander scale. Many professional meeting leaders would line the walls with flip chart sheets before the meeting, or even cover the walls with butcher paper, so that everything could be captured in one giant tapestry. It worked well except that, before it could serve as a summary of the meeting, someone still had to type it up or somehow reduce it down to size once the meeting was over.

The next generation was the whiteboard/copier. Everything displayed on the whiteboard could be duplicated on a copier that was built into the whiteboard. Some boards even provided multiple panels, with only one visible at a time, so everything did not have to be erased every time a panel was filled.

While this provided a decent summary of the meeting, someone thought "Wouldn't it be nice if instead of just being printed out, then erased, everything on the board could be stored directly in a PC, where it could be edited, printed, e-mailed, faxed, and even networked to distant sites?" That you can have right now. There are several commercially available whiteboards that are fully linked to PCs, such as the SMART Board shown in Figure 4. Anything on the whiteboard is also instantly in the computer, where it is processed the same way as any other information stored in the computer.

That gets everything from the whiteboard to the computer. How about getting everything from the computer to the whiteboard? At the present time, the solution is to project whatever is in the computer onto the whiteboard using an overhead projector and an LCD display panel. Recent products even eliminate the overhead projector; the LCD panel and projector are a single self-contained unit (see Figure 5). Significant advances in large-scale projection systems are in the laboratory now.

The disadvantage to projecting an image is that it does not make the projected image an actual part of what is on the whiteboard. When the computer is used for anything else other than projecting that one image, the image disappears from the board.

Our description in Chapter One of a future meeting in a high-tech meeting center assumes products that permit information to flow in both directions. Information from the whiteboard will go directly into the computer, and information from the computer will actually show up on the surface of the whiteboard. (One of the nice things about making this kind of prediction is that we do not have to figure out how to create the appropriate technology.)

Figure 4. The SMART Board—a PC-linked whiteboard.

Courtesy of SMART Technologies, Inc.

Figure 5. A PC projector used with a SMART Board.

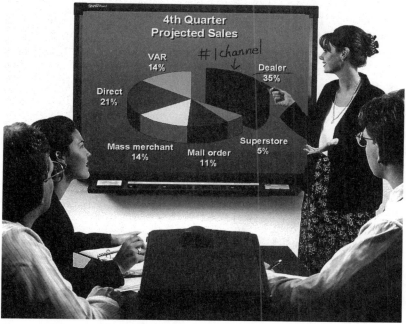

Courtesy of SMART Technologies, Inc.

Thin-Film Deposits on Walls

Our experience running scores of team meetings and our conversations with other experienced meeting facilitators indicate that when meetings get really creative and exciting, people are not sitting quietly at the table. They are up at the whiteboards, moving stuff around, drawing things, and generally making a lot of noise. Most meeting centers just assume that meeting room walls are part of the work space, and have coated the walls with whiteboard panels or some other surface that allows people to write and draw to their heart's content. One U.S. Army meeting center we visited has magnetized metal plates cut in all the familiar PERT-chart shapes. When planning a project, participants can write the step on an appropriately shaped metal plate, then move these steps around at will as the discussion goes on.

PC-linked whiteboards are a major step forward, but they are still a bit constraining in size. Wouldn't it be nice to be able to install the whiteboards as flat panels on the wall, so that the entire wall space of the room could be working space? Wouldn't it be nicer if instead of having to install panels, there was some kind of thin-film deposit we could put on the walls, so that the walls themselves would become PC-linked whiteboards?

Modeling/Holographic Projections

As long as we are being way out, it would also be nice if when an architect designed a building, people could actually walk around in a model and see what it looks like. Or, if a small group was working to design a product, it would be terrific if there was a model of it projected right onto the meeting room table. Better yet, when it came time to see how it worked, the group could see a 3-D simulation of how it would operate.

This may seem farther out than thin-film whiteboards, but the reality may be a lot closer. Contractors working for the U.S. Defense Department have constructed a meeting space in which holographic images can be projected. The images are sent from projectors at one end of the room, and meeting participants can see the image only by wearing special glasses. Originally the glasses were like goggles, but recently Texas Instruments has created viewing glasses that look like normal everyday reading glasses.

There will soon be little difficulty—using the multimedia technology just described above—to simulate actual processes within 3-D models. Groups will be able to make design changes on the spot and view the impact those changes will have on how the product works.

Remote Viewing Headgear

At present, doctors at medical centers in the United States can supervise heart surgery performed in other countries as it actually happens. The small video cameras used in desktop videoconferencing can be used to extend this concept greatly. The U.S. military has developed headgear incorporating miniaturized video cameras that broadcast information from the field back to headquarters. This means that commanders can make decisions based on immediate visual field information. Similarly, medics can wear headgear that shows battlefield wounds to surgeons back at a hospital. The first stage is to provide guidance to medics handling medical emergencies. The next stage, already under development, is for surgeons at a distance to perform actual operations using gloves that transmit the movements of their hands to robotic surgical equipment.

Remote viewing will be helpful anytime there are experts located in one place in the world who need to be able to actually see field conditions in another part of the world. Some of the uses of remote viewing might include discussion of production processes, handling of environmental problems, and assembling of intricate scientific equipment requiring several fields of expertise, and there are numerous applications for security.

Expert Systems

The handwriting software that permits you to write notes to your "personal digital assistant" (such as the Apple Newton) is based on its ability to learn. You are first asked to write out a sample of your handwriting, using a set of words that captures all the basic combinations of letters. Then you are asked to correct any mistakes the machine makes in reading your handwriting. At first the machine may make a number of mistakes. But it notes all the corrections, and steadily improves to nearly 100% recognition. But if somebody else writes to your machine, it has to start over learning that individual's handwriting.

What if you applied the same logic to understanding how an expert works? Most experts have developed a way of viewing problems that allows them to make rapid judgments on all but the most difficult problems. These ways of viewing things may include a systematic way of analyzing problems or a number of rules of thumb. Often, they show their true expertise by knowing when to break rules to solve the problem. What if you taught a computer all of an expert's rules or ways of thinking about problems, then you tracked the decisions made by the expert over time? Then, what if you recorded those decisions that could not be predicted based on the ground rules and learned from the expert why he or she made them? This would allow you to articulate additional rules, or be more specific about the conditions under which the rules do and do not apply.

If you did all this, you would have devised an **expert system**—a computer program that helps you replicate the approach that an expert would take to solving a problem. Rather than paying experts hundreds of thousands of dollars for advice, you could get the benefit of their wisdom for much less. Experts who complain they "can't be everywhere at once" would soon find they can be.

Expert systems will permit groups to have the cyber-expert right in the room with them during their meeting. Conceivably people will be able to access such systems over the Internet. The Internet will show home pages advertising various expert systems. When you want to use the expert system, you will be able to simply open up the home page, indicate the expert system you want to use, fill in a simple form for billing purposes, and run the program. Using an LCD presentation system, the program could be projected on a whiteboard, where the group could record its responses to the questions asked by the system. There would probably be some mechanism by which the group could report its results back to the expert system, so the system would learn from the group's experience.

Expert systems are being developed in virtually every field, although reliability of these systems is still being tested. Decisions ranging from how to direct elevators so as to avoid waits or processing of orders in warehouses to where to drill for oil may all soon be made by expert systems. All this "wisdom" can be brought directly into the meeting room over the Internet or an intranet.

Summing Up

The goal of much of the new technology is quite simply that people can participate "anytime, anyplace" and in any way that fits their level of interest. The new technology brings all the data from the outside world into the meeting room, for instant access. But it also makes it possible for people outside the room to observe and comment on what is going on in the room, again at their own level of interest.

But as exciting as the technology is, it's still only one component of an effective collaboration system. Let us turn next to equally important innovations in meeting process.

Note

1. Kenneth Boulding, Presentation to World Future Society, Second World Assembly, Washington, D.C., June 2–5, 1975.

6

Meeting Process

In recent years, the business world has rediscovered the difference in meaning between the words **task** and **process**. With simultaneous pressures to downsize yet provide dramatically improved customer service, organizations have found that simply trying to speed up performance or do the same tasks better will not do the job. The whole process by which decisions are made and tasks are performed must be reengineered.

A telephone company, for example, found that when a business customer called in to request phone lines, it took more than a month to activate those lines. When the company reengineered the process it found that 95% of the decisions that had to be made by a succession of specialists could be made instead by a single generalist. In fact, with a little work on its spare parts system, the generalist could handle 99% of all decisions. The generalists had to receive considerably more training and had to be supported by a sophisticated computer-based information system, but activation time was cut from 30 days to 4 hours. In addition, the generalists found their job much more interesting and rewarding because they were free to make decisions, and had the information to do so wisely. Experiences like this have greatly enhanced our understanding of the importance of process.

The difficulty with process is that it is normally inherent or embedded in the situation so that it goes unnoticed. In the terminology of technologists, it is transparent. Psychologists would call it unconscious.

To illustrate: The story is told that during World War II the British military was unhappy because it was unable to fire its artillery as rapidly as the manufacturer said it could. So it sent in an efficiency expert to see what was wrong. The efficiency expert listed each step, timed it, and evaluated whether the sequence made sense. Everything checked out except that after the guns had been loaded, the men who loaded the gun walked a few feet away and stood at attention. Since they wore goggles and ear protectors it was not clear why they walked away and stood at attention. But since the Army had been following the same drill for more than 100 years, the efficiency expert was hesitant to tell it to stop doing it until he understood why they were doing it in the first place. All was revealed when he had lunch with an old regimental commander, longtime retired. He explained the problem he was working on, to which the old commander responded: "That's simple, they've gone over to hold the horses."

Of course they had not had horses for nearly 40 years. But that's the point. Processes are ways of doing things that over time we have found get the job done. Rather than have to figure out how to get the job done each time we face it, we develop a routine that works well without having to think about it. Ordinarily, not having to think about the process results in a great savings of time and energy, but not when technology or priorities or external conditions change. Then, not being aware of process, just repeating tasks because that's the way it's always been done, can be a major handicap threatening organizational survival.

The high point of Molière's play *Le Bourgeois Gentilhomme* is when the nouveau riche gentleman discovers to his great satisfaction that he has been speaking in prose all his life. In much the same way, every meeting has a process, whether we are conscious of it or not. You cannot avoid using a process. The only choice you have is to use a process that's appropriate for your purposes.

In the 1950s and 1960s there was considerable experimentation with "totally unstructured meetings." The group would sit around waiting for something to happen, but when someone did suggest the group do something, this individual was roundly criticized for trying to structure the meetings—horror of horrors! Eventually people discovered that totally unstructured meetings were actually a very rigid, not to mention unproductive, form of meeting. The question to ask was not, How can we avoid structure? but, Which structure is appropriate for a specific circumstance? Process does matter, and it cannot be avoided. This has extremely important implications for meeting technologies. If designers of the new technology embed old process assumptions into the new technology, they are likely to limit the value of the new technology.

Group Process Innovations

Table 2 lists the group process innovations that were included in FutureTech's cybermeetings, discussed in Chapter One.
Here's a brief description of each of these innovations.

Facilitators

Since the 1970s, a whole new profession has grown up of people whose business it is to lead meetings. These individuals normally call themselves facilitators, to distinguish their neutrality on decisions being made in the meetings. Many organizations now use facilitators to conduct important meetings. Facilitators are likely to be used particularly for strategic planning sessions, team building, in support of project teams, or to assist with dispute resolution.

Facilitators are skilled in stimulating participation and in getting commitment from all participants to decisions made by the group. They are also skilled in making sure people feel included and understood, in handling dysfunctional behavior, and generally in creating a climate of psychological safety that makes it easy for people to participate openly and enthusiastically.

Facilitation is particularly appropriate when the objective is a group decision and group commitment to implementation.

Table 2. Group process ingredients of cybermeetings.

Meeting Process Innovations	*Current Status (1996)*
Facilitators	The terms *facilitator* and *facilitation* are widely used. Many organizations have trained their staff in facilitation skills. Use of third-party facilitators is usually limited to special meetings.
Meeting room walls as work space	Some general use to enhance group collaboration. Characteristic of most interactive meeting centers, or skunkworks. (For a discussion of skunkworks, see "Meeting Centers, or Skunkworks," in Chapter 7.)
Visual group memory	Keeping summaries on flip charts or whiteboards is widespread. Use of visual group memory is still limited.
Interactive group processes to improve group effectiveness	Interactive techniques to educate, stimulate innovation, and improve decision making are widely but not universally used.
Adapting a meeting's process to its purpose	Widely recommended in meeting training, but less universal in actual use. Process design is part of the services offered by professional facilitators.

(Continues)

Table 2. *(Continued)*

Meeting Process Innovations	Current Status (1996)
Graphic guides and process wizards	Presently used with large wall-size banners. Could readily be stored in a computer and projected onto the wall. PC-based process wizards linked to projector systems or whiteboards are on the market, and many more are in development. Use of wall-size templates is limited.
Meetingware	Several meetingware products are commercially available, many using keypad technology.
Team building to jump-start temporary teams	This tool for turning a collection of people into a team is in wide and increasing use.

It is less appropriate to heavily hierarchical organizations using top-down decision making. In hierarchical organizations, the highest-ranking person in the organization usually runs the meeting. This can produce many dysfunctional behaviors:

○ People's responses to the meeting leader may be dictated more by the desire to impress (or challenge) rather than the needs of the meeting.
○ When the boss suggests that a meeting move in a particular direction, or summarizes the discussion, this is interpreted as a decision, not a helpful suggestion.
○ When bosses make suggestions about how the meeting should be run, they are often seen as manipulating the meeting to produce a predetermined outcome—a

perception that may be accurate—rather than as working on behalf of the whole group's interests.

○ With high rewards and potential punishment at stake, some people will engage in appeasing, apple-polishing behavior toward the meeting leader. Others will withdraw into silence or will rebel, engaging in oppositional behavior.

○ Bosses often feel put on the spot when questions are raised about projects or decisions in which they played a role, and may respond defensively.

○ Bosses may signal that it is unsafe to talk about certain topics, even when those are exactly the problems that need to be addressed for the survival of the group.

If someone who is genuinely neutral leads the meeting, it is clearer that this person's action and suggestions are intended to help the meeting. This individual has little ability to reward or punish. Whatever authority the person has is given to him/her by the group, because the group wishes to succeed.

Some people worry that a leader who does not possess organizational status or rank will be unable to exert sufficient control to make the meeting a success. This concern does not check out in practice. In effect, there is a transaction in which the group grants the leader some authority to control the meeting, in return for the leader's not having an agenda about what the outcome of the meeting will be. The leader has a stake in the group's feeling that the meeting was successful, but not in a particular solution and decision.

The real power that a neutral meeting leader has is the power to help the group to be a success. As long as the group senses that the leader's actions are on behalf of the group's success, they will support the leader. The minute a facilitator is seen as being on an ego trip or having a personal agenda, he/she will be challenged.

Most organizations that use facilitation extensively have developed their own internal cadre of facilitators. They may use an external facilitator for a particularly important or controversial meeting, but everyday meetings are led by someone from within the organization who has received training in facilitation skills. Often this is done to save money. But it is also true that someone who is highly knowledgeable about the subject has an easier time tracking the conversation. The disadvantage of having people who are intimately familiar with a topic be the facilitator is that they are more likely to have an opinion about the topic, and have difficulty constraining themselves from getting involved in pushing a particular outcome. Once the neutrality on outcome is lost, their acceptability as a meeting leader is diminished.

There are definite skills required to be an effective facilitator, and normal management training does not usually provide training in these skills. There are facilitation training courses available, and most organizations that use facilitation extensively have internal training for supervisors, managers, and others who will serve as facilitators. This training is valuable not only for people who want to formally act as a facilitator but for all people who may find themselves leading meetings.

Facilitation skills are a core competency for companies organizing around temporary project teams or using any form of matrix management. Much of the challenge of getting people to work together is for team members to see that the structure is there to support their success, not to impose hierarchy. As the new cybermeeting technology comes on-line, the meeting leaders are far more likely to be chosen for their meeting leadership skills and ability to facilitate bringing people together than for their status and rank.

Meeting Room Walls as Work Space, and Visual Group Memory

We predict that in the future virtually all the walls of the meeting room will be considered work space. Gone will be the fancy art collections and mementos of past glories. That space is just too valuable for working!

At the simplest level, wall space is used to record ideas so they are not lost. Wall space can also be used to keep a summary of the meeting, particularly of any agreements reached. People want to be heard, and they want to be sure others got the message. Keeping a running summary displayed on the wall is a way of saying "We got it! Here it is!" Once the idea is up on the wall, people have less need to make the same argument, or escalate their comments in order to make themselves heard. People can verify that they had been understood with just a glance at the wall. Working on the wall, at a scale everybody can see and participate in, is a useful way of helping everybody visualize what is being said, and is also a way of creating the feeling of a shared group product.

Over the past several decades, people have been experimenting with walls precovered with flip chart or butcher paper. People quickly saw that ideas do not have to be recorded on the wall in sequence, with one comment being recorded right after another. Instead, it is possible to group related ideas together spatially. So an idea might emerge early in a meeting and not be mentioned for a while, then a similar or reinforcing idea might be expressed. If ideas are recorded in a linear manner, these ideas would be put on entirely different parts of the walls. But if the recorder recognizes the relationship between the ideas, and records them side by side, the participants can literally see the connections. Sometimes this helps participants understand new relationships between ideas: "Idea A is a precursor or early stage that leads to Idea B, with Ideas C, D, and E all being a subset of Idea B." Capturing this visually helps groups imagine entire processes in a way that would be almost impossible to do if people had to hold all those ideas in their heads.

The process of recording entire meetings on walls, showing related ideas, and relationships between ideas is often called **visual group memory.** There are trainers who specialize in training people to do this kind of visual recording and people who make a living providing this kind of recording service.

Inevitably, because it is a visual approach, professional recorders have moved from just verbal summaries to visual portrayals of processes, ideas, and people. Two of the leading practitioners of visual group memory, David Sibbett and Jim Channon, have been pioneering the use of quickly drawn cartoonlike illustrations built right into the summary. The constraint on this powerful technique has been that it required a talented artist with a flair for capturing concepts and presenting them visually, who also has extensive knowledge of group process.

In the future, computer assistance may remove these limitations. Millions of people with no artistic skill can now integrate professionally drawn graphics into their materials in just a few seconds by drawing on computer-based libraries of clip art. It will soon be possible to draw from computer-based libraries of visual symbols that meeting recorders can use to capture group discussions. A recorder who is not a trained artist will be able to project these symbols onto PC-connected working walls, providing a full visual summary.

Interactive Group Processes to Improve Group Effectiveness

Have you ever watched *Sesame Street* with one of your children or grandchildren? It's loud, noisy, hyperactive, and terribly stimulating. It's almost everything our own schooling was not. And it's much better teaching. *Sesame Street* and many other highly interactive educational programs for children model principles that apply equally well with adults:

- People learn more when they're more involved.
- People become committed through involvement.
- Involvement is increased with active participation and use of multiple senses.
- Interaction stimulates interest, enjoyment, and creativity.

The best motivational speakers know this. Watch them work a crowd. They will do almost anything to get people raising hands, shouting out answers, standing up, sharing experiences, and so on. They know that real understanding and changes in attitudes occur when people are interacting, not when they are sitting passively, like bumps on a log.

The simple reality is that if all the meetings in your organization are polite, prim, and proper, you are probably not getting the most out of your people. Real learning, creativity, and commitment are messy, noisy, and sometimes confusing.

Brainstorming and Other Idea-Generating Techniques

Facilitators and other designers of meetings have developed a whole repertoire of interactive techniques and processes designed to improve people's effectiveness during meetings. One of the simplest and best known of these processes is brainstorming. In brainstorming, participants are asked to generate long lists of possible solutions, without any judgmental comments or analysis. Only after the group is totally drained of ideas does it turn to evaluation.

This simple technique contains within it principles of great importance:

- ○ Creativity requires going beyond conventional boundaries.
- ○ Suspending analysis and evaluation is a necessary precondition for thinking about things in new ways.
- ○ Mental (and even physical) playfulness, without judgment, is a way of getting beyond boundaries.

A more advanced version of brainstorming is the use of analogies to direct thinking into new pathways. A problem in computer design may be solved by asking how the same problem is solved in a living organism.

Actually, research shows that while brainstorming is superior to processes where every idea is critiqued as it is presented, group brainstorming may not be as effective as getting a group to generate ideas individually (while sitting in a group, or electronically) and then to evaluate the ideas as a group. Researchers have noticed that when people use brainstorming they tend to develop ideas in reaction to each other's ideas. If you want to get people to take totally different approaches, have a period of silent generation of ideas, with each participant developing a long list. Then go around the group, with each person sharing one idea until everybody says "pass." The peer pressure of generating the ideas in a group makes people generate more ideas, but because ideas are generated silently, they do not all approach the problem the same way. By going around the circle, everybody feels like a participant. No idea is left unspoken because it does not seem to fit the consensus viewpoint.

Specialists in creativity training have developed a whole box of tricks designed to get people and groups outside of their normal linear, evaluative mode of thinking.[1] Doug Hall, the founder and president of Richard Saunders International, is a marketing whiz who has taken these concepts to new heights.[2] Hall is scornful of brainstorming, calling it "brain-draining." He invites product development and marketing teams to the Eureka Mansion in Cincinnati, where they work together with people from Hall's organization—called "trained brains"—to develop new marketing ideas. At the heart of Hall's approach is bombarding participants with stimuli in an atmosphere full of fun. Stiff, formal executives may soon find themselves in a nerf-ball war that loosens them up with each other and, Hall believes, also loosens up their thinking. Then the stimulus begins, including a number of playful processes designed to get the brain sparking. It seems to work. Many of America's largest corporations beat their way to Hall's mansion. Hall also cites research by Arthur VanGundy of the University of Oklahoma indicating that his high-stimulus approach produces many more ideas than brainstorming, and many of these ideas are of superior quality.[3]

Techniques for Reaching Mutual Agreements

Just as there are processes to stimulate creativity, experts on dispute resolution have developed processes or strategies for helping people reach mutual agreements.[4] For example, typically, negotiations start with people taking fixed positions, accompanied by accusations about how the other person's behavior has harmed them. This means the negotiations start out adversarial, win/lose, and usually go from there to worse.

A simple process for opening negotiations is to have people identify their interests, instead of their positions, then work together to identify criteria for what would be acceptable solutions. Again, this process contains important principles:

○ A fixed position is only one possible way to meet an individual's interest.
○ Once you get people talking about interests, it opens up many more directions for resolution.
○ Developing criteria together not only builds confidence, but because it is a shared activity, it builds the relationship between the parties.

Adapting a Meeting's Process to Its Purpose

A considerable body of process knowledge has grown up since the 1960s. (See the box on the next page for a summary of group process insights that can be used in running meetings.) With practice and training, people get better and better at using these processes. In organizations that use these processes, it is not unusual to go into a meeting room and find ground rules for a number of different processes, from brainstorming to strategic decision-making processes, posted on the walls. They serve as visual reminders to groups of the many useful interactive processes to increase meeting effectiveness.

Research shows that using these carefully designed structured processes does make a difference in group effectiveness. Charles Pavitt of the University of Delaware recently conducted a review of the group process research literature, looking only at those research studies that meet academic standards for acceptable research and looking for patterns across a number of studies rather than just individual study results. Among his key findings:

○ Nine of ten studies showed that when groups used a formal procedure rather than free discussion, and there was an objectively verifiable correct answer, the groups using the structured process were far more likely to come up with an accurate answer.

A FEW KEY PROCESS PRINCIPLES

Here are process principles that are useful when designing meetings:

○ Define the problem carefully *before* discussing solutions.

○ In a dispute, seek to understand each other's interests rather than take positions.

○ If people are upset, let them ventilate before trying to problem-solve—and be sure they feel understood before you try to move on.

○ Suspend judgment while you are generating options. Creativity requires a climate of psychological safety.

○ Group brainstorming is good, but silent individual brainstorming in the presence of a group may be better.

○ The more senses people engage in the learning process, the better they learn.

○ Participation is the direct path to commitment.

○ If you want big ideas, work big! Walls are work space, not decor.

○ Fix the problem, not the blame.

○ Decisions made using a formal discussion method result in higher decision quality—although the time spent making the decision may be longer.
○ Groups that use procedures are more satisfied with their decisions and more committed to their implementation.

○ The order of the steps does matter, particularly when seeking creative ideas. When evaluation and discussion of alternatives are mixed, for example, there are fewer total proposals and fewer good proposals.[5]

Graphic Guides and Process Wizards

When Creighton & Creighton ran a policy center, a highly interactive meeting space, for the U.S. Department of Labor, there was a long entrance corridor from the Secretary of Labor's offices into the policy center. One of the consultants came up with the bright idea of having a display along that wall, with each team visually portraying what it was working on and what progress was being made. This way, Secretary Robert Reich, who dropped in at the policy center periodically, could get a quick briefing on what was going on in the center as he walked down the corridor into the main work area.

We developed a kind of template for what each team would report, as shown in Figure 6. These templates are wall size, about 4 feet high and 12 feet long. Teams could "fill in the blanks" using a flow pen.

In reality, these templates were never used the way we anticipated. Instead, the teams wanted to keep them in their work area as a way of tracking their own progress and as a visual reminder of agreements reached.

The templates solved another problem. The original plan was that when each new team entered the policy center they would go through a team building/strategic planning session conducted by one of our professional facilitators. In fact, budget constraints made it impossible to provide a facilitator for every team, and we soon found that most teams—at least those that weren't having major interpersonal problems—were able to have a successful team building session without a professional facilitator by using these process templates as the structure for the session.

We have been experimenting with the use of process templates for several years now. Our experience to date is that a great deal of process wisdom can be embedded in the template, so that the need for a professional facilitator is lessened. The process templates also ensure a minimum standard of

Figure 6. A strategic planning process chart developed for the U.S. Department of Labor skunkworks.

process quality, which can be improved upon if the group receives facilitation help or possesses its own facilitation skills.

David Sibbett of Grove Consultants International has worked with a similar concept for a number of years, calling his wall-size charts Graphic Guides®. Sibbett believes that graphic guides encourage big-picture thinking, show an entire system on one chart, and invite group participation. Sibbett has developed an entire library of graphic guides for different purposes. Figure 7 shows a group guide for strategic planning, while Figure 8 is a group guide for analyzing waves of techno-logical innovation.

The next step is to combine the idea of graphic guides with a computer to produce what we have called process wiz-ards. If you have used presentation software (such as Mi-crosoft's PowerPoint or Corel's Persuasion) to prepare a pre-sentation using overheads, you may remember that you were

Figure 7. Journey Vision Graphic Guide®.

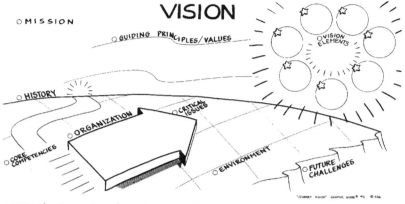

©1996 The Grove Consultants International.

given the option of selecting a "Look Wizard." The Look Wizard allows you to make a few simple choices, and suddenly your presentation is formatted. Had you done the formatting yourself, it would have taken a lot more time. More important, it would have taken a lot more knowledge about how to use the software.

Since presentation software is not the kind of software

Figure 8. Industry Structure Graphic Guide®.

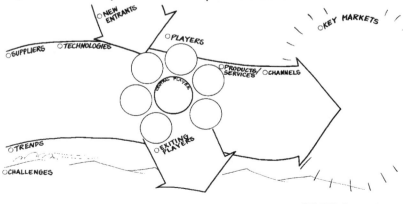

©1996 The Grove Consultants International.

most people use every day, most people do not take the time to master it. They are grateful to let the wizard do the working. Embedded in the wizard is a great deal of expert knowledge. But for most people there is no reason to acquire all that knowledge. They just want to accomplish their task in the quickest, most direct manner.

Similarly, the use of process templates could be greatly expanded if a team could select from a menu of templates, each designed to serve a different process need. These templates could then be projected onto a PC-connected whiteboard, where they could be filled in, with the responses stored in the computer so they could be printed out or faxed to others.

At present, process templates are just a promising idea. We expect to see the idea flourish when combined with the new technology.

Meetingware

There are already a number of electronic meeting tools, or meetingware, designed to utilize group process technologies in the meeting room setting. The September 1995 issue of *The Facilitator*, a quarterly publication of the Organization for Professional Facilitation, listed more than 25 such applications, with prices ranging from $295 to $15,000 (for up to 99 participants). By now there are undoubtedly many more.

Most of these applications are built around two capabilities made possible by technology: simultaneous (and anonymous) generation of ideas, and use of keypads for scoring or rating. For example, if everybody has a keyboard or electronic slate at their seat, a facilitator can pose a question and everyone can write ideas that then show up on the screen or whiteboard. This has several advantages: There's no additional time spent writing ideas up on the wall; people can generate ideas without being unduly influenced by each other's ideas; there's anonymity, so people can surface ideas without fear of disapproval or censure for "talking out of school" or otherwise goring sacred cows.

Then keypad technology can be used to rank the ideas,

do confidence checks ("What's your confidence on a scale of 1 to 9 that we will successfully implement the strategies as presented?"), or complete decision analysis weightings. Keypads are handheld wireless remotes given to each participant in the meeting. Typically they have a small LCD panel, a keyboard with ten numbers, *yes* and *no* keys, and a light that confirms that the participant's response has been received. They are particularly useful for evaluating, voting, or prioritizing. Groups that have used them say they eliminate a lot of time spent in such mundane tasks as tallying votes or recording weightings. They are often helpful in getting to a consensus, because people's preferences can be quickly expressed and the whole group can see which ideas can be accepted and which cannot. These systems are good at showing the group what they think, without the "mating dance" that often happens before people will engage difficult decisions. They also ensure that everybody participates.

Meetingware can also be used for electronic focus groups, with participants giving their numeric reactions to a presentation moment by moment. Following the presidential campaign debates between Bill Clinton and Robert Dole in 1996, *Newsweek* magazine published a story displaying reactions of a focus group to key sentences during the debate.

If everybody at the table were wired together electronically, then the keypad could be eliminated because everybody could simply respond on their keyboard. This has the advantage that there are virtually no limits to the number of people who could participate. Literally thousands of people could submit ideas or rank priorities via their desktop teleconferencing. People could be anywhere in the world and still participate.

A number of the meetingware applications have built in decision analysis processes as well, since the technology lends itself to eliciting scores or ratings from participants, analyzing them almost instantly, and presenting a display back to all participants simultaneously. Others permit the group to construct its own simulation of a process or system, then test outcomes using different assumptions. Many combine several processes. Council, one of the more widely used meetingware tools, provides two different processes for generating ideas, as well as tools for ranking, voting, and prioritizing.

To date, none of those tools is a "killer application"—a software tool like VisiCalc, the first spreadsheet for PCs[6]—which makes everybody feel they just have to have the technology so they can use the new application. Also, the probable direction for meetingware is that these tools will be built into an integrated package of options that are a part of each employee's desktop when they first open up their computer. They will be able to move directly to a process wizard that asks them a few questions, then routes them directly to process tools they can use to solve their particular problem. Microsoft already has a meeting design wizard built into its Office software package. It's likely that in the future specialized tools such as this will not be stored on individual PCs but will be stored on the server computer or even on the Internet for instant downloading when needed.

Team Building to Jump-Start Temporary Teams

The harsh reality, often ignored in the current rush to create temporary project teams, is that you cannot make a group of people a team just by telling them they are. In fact, as management consultants Katzenbach and Smith point out in their very wise book *The Wisdom of Teams*, the worst possible outcome of all the emphasis on teams is to create what they call pseudo-teams. Pseudo-teams are groups of people who believe they should be a team, share the rhetoric of being a team, but do not genuinely engage in shared, collaborative work. The rhetoric about being a team can be just enough to disrupt individual performance—so that individuals no longer feel free to act—without substituting effective teamwork. You can end up with the worst of all worlds: individuals who feel inhibited by their obligations to the team, while the team itself is not genuinely productive.[7]

The reality is that most effective teams get that way from working together closely for a prolonged time. Furthermore, the team experience is heightened if there is an external reality that increases the sense of urgency and raises the importance of the task to near-survival level.

Teams form quickly in war, in competitive sports, and when the survival of the organization is at stake. People often look back at an experience in an effective team with wonderment. There is no way they would want to go back to the pressure they experienced and the hours they worked in the team. But they often describe their experience as one of the most important of their lives, a period during which their senses seemed heightened and they felt more alive.

But how do you turn a group of people into a team in a hurry, on a project that is important but not life-threatening? Is there some way to jump-start the process?

Many organizations have found team building an effective tool for speeding up the formation of teams and increasing the effectiveness of existing teams. For some organizations team building has been around so long it seems commonplace. But it is still a departure for many.

Team building is a workshop usually held off-site and attended by all members of the team and lasting 2 days to a week. Team building sessions may include discussions that might occur in a typical business meeting, such as a strategic planning or visioning exercise. But one of the distinguishing characteristics of a team building session is the time spent on building relationships and developing group norms for communication within the team.

Whenever two people communicate, they communicate information but they also communicate about the relationship, that is, how much they accept, value, or trust each other. If you think of political arguments you have had that were fun and invigorating, not unpleasant, it was probably with someone with whom there was a long-standing relationship. It might have been a family member, an old schoolmate, or a childhood friend, but you knew that no matter what ridiculous positions you took, you would care about each other when the argument was over.

When there is trust, a strong relationship, it is possible to have strong disagreements over content or information and continue to work together effectively. But when that trust is not there, things are edgy and uncertain because the position you take may determine whether or not you are accepted or valued.

Much of the focus in team building is on strengthening the relationship. This may be done in several ways. One approach is the shared physical challenge approach of which the Outward Bound organization is a leading proponent. Team members participate in a physical challenge, such as climbing a cliff, white-water rafting, surviving in a wilderness area, and so forth, in the process building enhanced trust and respect for each other.

The other major, and more frequent, approach is to participate in group activities during which people talk more about who they are apart from their professional roles, or increase their openness about their emotional reactions to each other.

While the "encounter group" version of team building may have largely run its course, the reason encounter groups had value for many people is that trust is based on knowing and being known by each other. It's not based on head knowledge—it's far more visceral.

Under the tutelage of a skilled facilitator, teams can profit greatly from activities that emphasize knowing each other as people, not as role players but as human beings. This does not require the emotional extremes that occurred in some encounter groups. But it does require opening up beyond the comfort zone that usually exists around the office. After all, this is exactly what occurs under war conditions or in competitive sports. Team members share an intense experience during which they really come to see each other as human beings, not as performers of functions or roles.

It's already clear that while certain kinds of transactions can be handled via electronic media, others cannot. Building trust is something that, in the authors' experience, must be handled in person. Once that trust is built, then electronic communication may be quite satisfactory.

If meetings increasingly occur electronically, then the increasingly rare time that is spent face-to-face will become even more valuable. The skills of team building may be even more crucial in the future, so that when teams do get together physically they build sufficient trust in their relationships to make electronic communication successful the rest of the time.

Summing Up

The single most important principle from the group process field is to take responsibility for your meeting process. Most meetings are conducted the way they are because that's the way meetings have always been. Just as organizations are having to reengineer their manufacturing processes and their customer satisfaction processes, organizations need to make conscious choices about their meeting processes. A meeting process that is highly effective for one purpose may be totally ineffective for another. Without careful analysis of what the situation requires and how the meeting process matches those requirements, organizations will frequently have ineffective meetings without even knowing why. Worse, organizations may invest in expensive technologies that are designed to improve collaboration, only to use them in ways that discourage it.

Many people who are fascinated by innovative meeting technologies show great reluctance in considering group process innovation as having equal significance. They dismiss it with the claim that it is all just "touchy-feely," something that makes you feel good but does not have much substance. Their underlying premise seems to be that it's just designed to make people feel good, but it does not really change anything.

Our experience is that the new technologies and group process innovations work hand in hand. The new technologies provide a number of significant enabling tools for people in meetings. But the group process work also provides important insights into how to structure the technology so that people work together more effectively.

We turn now to the final component of the collaboration system, the facility itself.

Notes

1. Roger von Oech, *A Whack on the Side of the Head* (Menlo Park, Calif.: Creative Think, 1982); Michelle Ray and Rochelle Myers, *Creativity in Business* (New York: Doubleday, 1986); Richard Fobes, *The Creative Problem Solver's Toolbox* (Corvallis, Oreg.: Solutions through Innovation, 1993).
2. Doug Hall with David Wecker, *Jump Start Your Brain* (New York: Warner Books, 1995).
3. See Arthur VanGundy, *Idea Power* (New York: AMACOM, 1992), and Arthur VanGundy, *Brain Boosters for Business Advantage* (San Diego: Pfeiffer & Co., 1994).
4. For a simple summary of much of the best thinking in the field, see Roger Fisher and William Ury, *Getting to Yes* (Boston: Houghton Mifflin, 1981).
5. Charles Pavitt, "What (Little) We Know About Formal Group Discussion Techniques: A Review of Relevant Research," *Small Group Research*, vol. 24, no. 2 (May 1993), pp. 217–235.
6. For a fascinating discussion of the role VisiCalc played in the original acceptance of the personal computer, see Robert X. Cringely, *Accidental Empires* (New York: HarperBusiness, 1992).
7. Jon R. Katzenbach and Douglas K. Smith, *The Wisdom of Teams* (New York: HarperCollins, 1994).

7

Facility Innovations

"Meeting space itself *is* a form of groupware," according to Matt and Gail Taylor, who have designed a number of interactive meeting centers. Meeting facilities may either support and sustain new kinds of meetings, or constrain and restrict them. Just as new behaviors are needed to get maximum benefits from the new electronic and group process technologies, new facilities are needed to support new ways of working together collaboratively. But to understand these new facilities, it helps to start with the changing uses of work space.

The New Office Space

To predict where office space is headed, we explored what America's leading-edge high-tech firms are thinking when they design their research and development facilities. We are aware that many organizations have very different characteristics than a high-tech company, and the requirements of an R&D facility may be very different from those of a conventional office even within the same organization. But we believe that what's happening in Silicon Valley may be a harbinger of the future because (1) Silicon Valley's R&D facilities are being built for "knowledge workers," the growing sector of business; (2) trends there are more visible: Silicon Valley is building new facilities while many more established organizations are cutting back on office space; and (3) the newer, but successful, companies are often more likely to be the early adopters of innovations that will soon affect all businesses.

Here are some of the important trends in office design in Silicon Valley's high-tech companies:

○ *Offices are designed for productivity, not just cost, and not to communicate rank or status.* The starting place among the leading facility managers in Silicon Valley is to ask, How can the workplace contribute to organizational performance?[1] They want to go beyond cost reduction to create increased value. They believe the workplace is a tool that—along with many other factors—affects productivity. Done well, it makes a contribution. Done poorly, it detracts.

This is not just a feel-good goal. Michael Brill, an architect and office space researcher who exerts considerable influence on Silicon Valley thinking, asserts that based on his research it is reasonable to believe that good office design can produce an across-the-board productivity increase of 5% of salary annually for workers in all job categories. Brill's research shows increases in the range from 3% to 20%, but he believes the 5% figure is realistic.[2]

At the core of this approach is what Brill calls "skeptical analysis," a fundamental reexamination of all assumptions about how facilities work. One of the assumptions that is sure to be challenged is the idea that offices are designed primarily to communicate status or rank. With some exceptions, Silicon Valley facility planners veer away from the "ego trip office." Ego trips do not show up on the bottom line.

A number of companies lean toward what has been called **universal officing,** so called because everyone, regardless of status, has identical space. This is a concept pioneered by the hugely successful Intel Corporation. Senior executives have offices identical to most workers. There are no reserved parking spaces. There are no executive dining rooms. Intel thrives on its self-described "paranoia" that it will be caught unawares and surpassed by a significant technological advance. It believes it cannot afford the trappings of hierarchy because those trappings have an impact upon people's willingness to communicate openly. If a junior engineer fails to tell the senior vice president that she is wrong, because he is overawed by her status and the regalia of her office, the company may miss the boat and fall behind. So the rule is not to do things that exaggerate differences between people.

While not many high-tech companies have adopted a policy as pure as Intel's, the emphasis in Silicon Valley is on performance. If the job you perform requires that there be a small meeting space in your office, you will get it (but you will probably share it). You will not get it just because of rank.

○ *Offices are used, not owned, by their occupants—they're more like a hotel.* The occupants of Silicon Valley's offices are the embodiment of what is meant by the term *knowledge worker.* Rather than engage in repetitive tasks, their job is to innovate, to create, and to interact. Knowledge workers use their offices very differently than office workers performing routine tasks. An increasing number of knowledge workers do not even come to work—they "commute" electronically.

Knowledge workers have very different use patterns. These patterns can be described as:

—Mostly in
—Mostly out
—In and out often
—Out long

Workers who are mostly in need an office that is assigned to them personally, that they can call their own. Workers who are in and out often also need an assigned office so they can work efficiently on the fly. But more than that they need a communication system that allows their coworkers to reach them wherever they are. Workers who are mostly out do not need a permanent office. They need storage for their files (most of which will increasingly be electronic anyway) and a place to work those few times they are in. They also need a communication system that reaches them wherever they are. Workers who are out long need an assigned office when they are in, but when they are gone, that office space is wasted unless someone else uses it. But they need the communication link wherever they are.

Michael Brill has concluded, based on his research, that *shared offices do not work*. When both people are in, neither can work productively. One of the occupants usually ends up using another space temporarily, losing access to his or her telephone, files, and resource materials.

What does work is to operate offices much like a hotel. People do not own an office while they are out, but they get an excellent one when they are in. Brill proposes the following general rules for what he describes as periodic residents (which he believes to be up to one fourth of the workforce):

—Provide first-rate tools, administrative support, and high-performance workplaces for when they need to be *in* the office.

—Provide a secure home base to store their belongings while they are gone, where other people can drop things off, and where they can drop in to work occasionally.

—Provide a single telephone number that follows residents wherever they go. Location should be transparent to colleagues and clients.

—Ensure parity of accommodations with people who are mostly in. Being a periodic resident is not second-class citizenship.

—Make it easy to return to the office, find what they need, and get to work *fast*.

—Help people feel and stay connected to the organization and their colleagues as they come in and out of the office.[3]

A number of these ground rules hold true for meeting spaces as well. Even though meeting spaces are normally used on a temporary basis, they too need to provide first-rate tools and administrative support and should be a high-performance workplace. They also need to provide a transparent communication link back to home base, whether it is an office, a car, or a home.

○ *The unit of performance is teams, not just individual workers.* Increasingly the focus of design is teams, not individuals. As people are out of the office more and more work is being done in teams, the actual size of individual offices in Silicon Valley is getting smaller. But more space is being designed for use by the team as a unit.

Professor Wellford Wilms of the UCLA Graduate School of Education and Information Systems has conducted a number of studies looking at how teams perform effectively. After looking at teams as varied as auto workers at the New United Motors plant in Fremont, California, and senior scientists at Hewlett-Packard's R&D laboratories, Wilms concludes that while some teams work in spite of their context, whether it be the management culture or tools and processes, teams that thrive do so because their social and physical environments provide nurturing conditions for them. The question, of course, is, What kind of physical environment provides these nurturing conditions.[4]

Researchers believe that teams do need an identifiable space that gives them a "group address" and a sense of identity. Teams, even temporary teams, need a place where they can leave team stuff. Teams need space to hang large charts and display schedules, tasks, or processes. They also need space for team socializing, an essential element in forming team identity.

○ *Work space must protect "the flow."* The Institute of Research in Learning (IRL) recently analyzed a software group at Sun Microsystems and determined that there are at least three distinct phases to developing new software products: There is a period of intense interaction as the team defines the customer requirements and specifications; there is a solitary period during which individual developers write the software, a period requiring intense concentration and lack of interruption; and finally another interactive period as the team integrates all the pieces and tests the software.[5]

Similar experiences are reported by other high-tech companies. All of them are concerned with protecting "the flow."[6] In normal language we talk about interrupting the flow of conversation or interrupting the chain of thought. This becomes a highly significant consideration in creative work. As Tom DeMarco describes it in his book *Peopleware:* "Flow is a condition of deep, nearly meditative involvement. Not all work roles require that you attain a state of flow in order to be productive, but for anyone involved in engineering, design, writing and like tasks, flow is a must. These are high momentum tasks. It's only when you're in flow that the work goes well."[7]

There is a continuing debate in Silicon Valley between those companies favoring individual offices and those favoring open office space with cubicles created with movable partitions. Hewlett-Packard was one of the creators of the open office concept, believing that it led to significantly improved communication and employee interaction. But in its new facilities even Hewlett-Packard provides "focus rooms" that are available on an as-needed basis for concentrated tasks. Social behavior also changes at open office companies. Employees at open office companies like 3Com, Cadence, and Oracle modulate their voices and behavior in the open spaces. Voices are kept low. Speaker phones are not used, and meetings that might disturb others are moved to meeting rooms.

Another option is Steelcase's Personal Harbor, a small cylindrical booth with a door that can be closed. There is enough room inside for a work surface, computer setup, a file drawer, and other standard desk items. There is also a whiteboard and CD player. Because the Harbor is circular, the actual space feels much larger than it actually is.

Adobe recently completed a new office facility in which it chose not to use the open space concept it used in its other facilities and instead opted for individual offices. One of the arguments for returning to individual offices was that it reduced the status difference between employees in open space and those few executives with offices.

○ *Encourage serendipity.* Many Silicon Valley R&D facilities are now being designed to encourage informal social interaction because the Valley's high-tech companies have learned that a chance encounter may produce the essential cross-fertilization of ideas that leads to a breakthrough.

Meeting Spaces

The three facility innovations reported in Chapter One included: (1) use of interactive meeting rooms; (2) integrating project work space with interactive meeting rooms; and (3) designing informal social spaces to encourage informal and serendipitous interactions.

Interactive Meeting Rooms

Different meeting purposes require different meeting room configurations. Yet most meeting spaces are designed as if one space fits all. Since the space must be used for a number of purposes, the space tends to be suitable for the lowest common denominator. Walls are decorated primarily for aesthetics; they are rarely thought of as work space. The room may contain a single whiteboard or easel. The facilities management department has made all the choices about furniture, and often there are strict rules about moving any of the furniture. The participants' only area of choice is in which meeting room they choose to meet.

The more established the organization, the more likely the meeting space will be luxuriously furnished, sedate, and designed to present an aura of restrained success—all qualities that tend to discourage interaction. People do not feel comfortable messing up such formally decorated space. Interactive work is messy. People tack drawings and plans on walls. They leave materials and computers in the room.

Leading meeting space designers design spaces that permit quick configuration of space for different purposes, and to accommodate entirely different kinds of meetings. The key concept is to design meeting space as a way to encourage and support collaboration. Virtually all walls—except the outside walls of the building—are movable. Interactive processes in particular require flexible spaces and the ability to adapt these spaces, in real time, as groups progress through different stages.

Leading meeting room designers suggest these guidelines:

1. *Make the space easy to configure to the needs of the team, minute to minute, day to day.* Create a neutral space that does not require a single room configuration. Get the tables and desks out of the way or put all furniture on wheels, making items easily movable, with teams encouraged to move them however they need to. Preferably, even the walls are on wheels, so the room can be completely adapted to the needs of the team.

2. *Work big.* Big ideas do not fit neatly on legal pads. Walls are work space because teams can think big and see whole processes. All walls have built-in whiteboards or work surfaces. Ideally the walls are curved, because they maximize viewing space and bring the materials on the wall closer to the participants.

3. *Make the space entertaining to the mind.* Provide a mix of the soothing and the colorful. Have engaging colors and forms. Make the space diverse and intriguing. Stock the environment with music, articles, posters, toys, books, and surprises.

4. *Provide large group interaction space and small breakout areas for small work groups and personal work.* Effective teams work in ways that look a lot like soap bubbles: They coalesce for one task, break apart into small groups, reconfigure into large but different arrangements, and break apart yet again. The meeting space needs to permit all these kinds of interaction. Breakout spaces do not need to be separate rooms, so long as the space suggests coziness for a small group and has reasonable noise protection. Open small group spaces maximize the potential for cross-fertilization between small work groups.

Meeting Centers (or Skunkworks)

The kind of meeting space described in Chapter One—with electronic whiteboards, full-wall videoconferencing, and holographic projection—is expensive. Meeting rooms like this will not be located on every floor in every building. More likely they will be in centralized meeting centers designed for longer or particularly important meetings. This way they will get the usage that justifies the expense.

Another way to justify the expense is to build meeting centers that are designed not only for the ordinary meeting of several hours or a day, but also for use by project teams that may be working together for several weeks or even months.

Often these spaces are called skunkworks. The term *skunkworks* comes from Lockheed Aircraft. In the period after World War II, Lockheed came to realize that trying to design airplanes using the normal bureaucratic approach just was not working. Instead, Lockheed gathered up some of the brightest and best (but occasionally maverick) people from each of the crucial organizational units, and put them together in a single building, where they were given the authority they needed to make decisions about plane design.

Although the group was officially known as something like the Advanced Design Laboratory, it was known informally by everybody as the skunkworks because the building in which it was housed was across the street from an odiferous factory. The name was borrowed, in slightly modified form, from a very popular newspaper comic strip of that time called "L'il Abner," in which a moonshine still was referred to affectionately as "The Skonkworks." Despite the odor or the name, the Lockheed skunkworks produced many of the most famous military planes in the postwar era.

The term *skunkworks* is now used to describe a facility where temporary project teams are brought together to work on a project for a short but intense period of time. The facility Creighton & Creighton operated for the U.S. Department of Labor in Washington, D.C., during 1995 is representative (although some of its promise was never realized due to budget constraints). The facility was designed so that several teams would be housed there at the same time. During the year Creighton & Creighton operated the facility there were teams involved in drafting proposed legislation regarding displaced ("downsized") workers and long-term worker education. There were also teams developing policies in such areas as workplace ergonomics, steel erection standards, tuberculosis, child labor, and drugs in the workplace.

The facility was located in a much larger space occupied by the assistant secretary for policy and his staff. The assistant secretary's staff consisted largely of senior policy advisers with high levels of technical expertise in various areas of Department of Labor programs. They were housed in permanent offices that surrounded a very large open space that was officially known as The Policy Center but uniformly referred to as the skunkworks. Around the outer perimeter of this space were approximately 20 workstations, created by movable partitions. Each workstation contained the latest computer equipment, loaded with software including Lotus Notes, which at the time represented the state-of-the-art collaborative work software. The configuration of workstations was based on the needs of the team using the space. Some teams wanted to work together in common rooms, to increase interaction; others required isolated workstations. Typically there were three to four small teams occupying the space at any one time. Several stations were occupied by Creighton & Creighton staff who provided logistics support (sometimes 24 hours a day) and also could arrange for facilitation or other group process support.

The workstations surrounded another space, still quite large, which was the meeting space. Although declining federal budgets never permitted the Department of Labor to configure this space in accordance with plans that were developed, it was intended to be space that could be reconfigured in a very short time into meeting spaces serving the needs of several teams operating simultaneously. Plans called for partitions on wheels, with much higher than normal work space walls that would define the meeting spaces. These partitions would not only define the space visually but would serve as sound barriers and work space for the group. Virtually all the movable partitions would be lined with whiteboards, so that even though they were just rolled into place, they would provide the same work areas as a fixed wall.

In a plan laid out by architect Langdon Morris, there would be a large meeting area, called the Forum, which could be set up theater style for up to 70 people, or with a conference table for 16 people (see Figure 9). Four other project rooms

Figure 9. The Langdon Morris skunkworks conceptual floor plan for the U.S. Department of Labor.

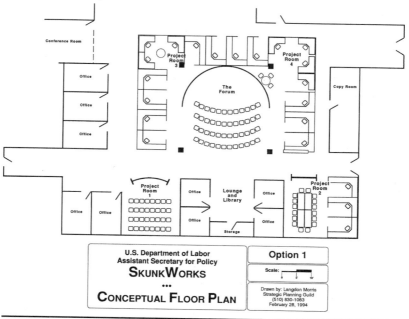

Design by Langdon Morris, Strategic Design Network, San Ramon, CA. ©1994 Langdon Morris. Reprinted with permission.

could be quickly configured for a smaller theater-style audience, for meetings around a conference table, or for shared office space.

Each team entering the skunkworks was asked to sign an agreement spelling out how long it intended to stay there, the number of team members that were to be housed there, the logistics support it would need (some teams brought their own), and the facilitation and group process support it wanted. The assistant secretary's policy staff were also available, either to serve as members of the teams or as consultants to the teams, as the teams wished.

The size of the teams tended to shrink and swell depending on where they were with their project. As a result, a certain number of workstations were assigned on a "hotelling" basis, meaning that they would be reserved in advance for several days. The "guest" would use the workstation as if it were his or her own office for the reserved period. But immediately upon his or her departure, a new nameplate was put up and somebody else occupied the space.

Periodically the teams reached a point in development of policies or draft legislation where they felt the need for feedback from interested parties and stakeholder groups. The skunkworks would then be reconfigured to host meetings of up to 100 people. In addition, videoconferencing equipment was brought into the facility to permit comments from regional offices, or to permit Secretary Reich to make major announcements to the field. This facility was using technologies available in 1993, and even then was budget constrained. Several private corporations have comparable or superior facilities using much more of the technology described earlier in this chapter.

One of people's concerns about interactive meeting centers, particularly with movable partitions and multiple teams, is noise. This is increasingly a solvable problem. New **noise-masking technology** will permit very different activities within a single meeting center. Noise-masking technology reduces sounds by broadcasting matching sound waves that effectively cancel both sources of noise. Other technologies that can be manipulated and adapted to specific meeting purposes include mood/attitude enhancement and heat, light, humidity, and other comfort controls.

Team Space

As noted above, the current trend is to shrink the size of individual offices, or even to have individuals share offices through hotelling arrangements, but there is a compensatory need for more team space. A *Business Week* article from April 29, 1996, provided an example of this kind of space, in the executive suite at the Aluminum Company of America: "Everyone in the new executive suite, secretary and CEO alike, works in cubicles without permanent walls or doors, gathering in a 'communications center' with tables, TVs, and a fax machine or nuking [microwaving] take-out [food] in a kitchen-

Table 3. Facility ingredients of cybermeetings.

Facility Features	Current Status (1997)
Interactive meeting rooms	A number of prototypes exist, and the concept is spreading.
Project work space integrated with interactive meeting rooms—the skunkworks concept	There are a growing number of examples, but the practice is not yet widespread.
Informal social spaces designed to encourage informal and serendipitous interactions, e.g., hearths, team kitchens	Currently part of the design specifications for a number of high-tech companies, particularly for R&D facilities.

ette." CEO Paul H. O'Neill says that his favorite hangout is the kitchen: "It's like being at home in your own kitchen and sitting around the table." At present this experiment is only on the top floor, where the executives are, but O'Neill plans to bring this style of working space to the entire company.

A number of organizations are going to small office spaces surrounding open spaces that can serve as either meeting space or social space, and that provide large walls that permit people to diagram complex projects or designs (see Table 3). Other organizations are designing small spaces, scattered throughout their buildings, that are just right for a handful of people to gather round "the hearth" and share coffee and conversation. Many of the R&D campuses in Silicon Valley have elaborate cafeterias and dining rooms, open to all employees, specifically to encourage interaction across organizational lines.

The Changing Role of the Facility Manager

These new trends in office and meeting space design—away from cookie-cutter operations with a little overlay of aesthetics—imply a changing and far more exciting role for facility managers. Facility managers will be concerned not only with cost reduction but with improving productivity. They will become students of group behavior, to discover which designs encourage collaboration and improve productivity. On the other hand, facilities managers will have to give up control over how the space will be configured. Meeting spaces need to be shaped to suit the purpose of the meeting, not of the facility manager.

Summing Up

Meeting rooms are not neutral. They can either encourage and enhance productivity or they can inhibit it. Future meeting rooms will be designed so that groups can work on the walls, with electronic technology augmenting participants' ability to visualize options and processes and to record the discussion and agreement. The room and its furnishings will be designed so that participants can reconfigure them instantly to meet their purposes. Meeting rooms will no longer be designed to connote status. Instead they will encourage interaction and empower their users.

Meeting space is no longer confined to meeting rooms. Facility designers are designing team space throughout buildings. These spaces will give teams a sense of team identity and a home base they "own" and can use to fit their needs, and will provide opportunities for the kind of socializing that strengthens bonds between team members. Even those spaces that are not for team use will be designed to encourage chance encounters and support enthusiastic discussions wherever people happen to meet in the building. Rather than prohibit socializing, management will recognize that socializing plays an important role in getting information across organizational lines. Breakthroughs may emerge from such chance encounters.

This discussion of facilities completes our discussion of four of the basic components of cybermeetings—organizational culture, meeting technology, meeting process, and meeting facilities. We turn next to how to decide which collaborative technologies are right for your organization.

Notes

1. Joe Akinori Ouye et al., "The Workplace as a Performance Tool," R&D Workplace Productivity Consortium, 1996. Members of the Consortium include 3Com, Adobe Systems, Bay Networks, Cadence Design Systems, Cisco Systems, Hewlett-Packard, NetScape, Octel Communications, Oracle, Sun Microsystems, and Tandem Computers.
2. Michael Brill, "Now Offices, No Offices, New Offices . . . Wild Times in the World of Office Work," *Technion*, no date.
3. Ibid.
4. Wellford Wilms, Professor of Education and Information Science, University of California at Los Angeles, presentation to the September 8, 1994, meeting of the R&D Workplace Productivity Consortium.
5. Christopher Darpuzet et al., *Rethinking "Distance" in Distance Learning* (Menlo Park, Calif.: Institute for Research on Learning, IRL Report No. 19.101, May 1995).
6. Mihaly Csikszentmihalyi, *Flow: The Psychology of Optimal Experience* (New York: HarperCollins, 1991).
7. Tom De Marco and Timothy R. Lister, *Peopleware: Productive Projects and Teams* (New York: Dorset House Publishing, 1987), p. 63.

8

Deciding Which Collaborative Innovations to Use

The last three chapters have presented an array of innovations in meeting technology, process, and facilities, all designed to increase collaboration in your organization. There are so many useful innovations, you may be asking: When should each innovation be used? Under what circumstances?

The results of research on when and how to use the technologies are just coming in. Some of the findings are anecdotal, but still useful. For example, researchers at an IBM "meeting room of the future" make the following observations about the use of videoconferencing:

○ People prepare for electronic meetings more carefully.
○ Electronic presentations are more disciplined.
○ This discipline generally makes electronic meetings more effective.
○ People do get more comfortable with the technology.

But they also note that electronic format and videoconferencing work less well:

○ With those who are first-time users, unfamiliar with using the technology

Type of Involvement	Technology Used
The customer team member could request market evaluations from his/her home office.	Same as above.
The team could provide an opportunity for senior management to monitor progress.	Management could access team progress by checking in with the team's home page on the intranet.
The team could have other staff develop prototypes of products under consideration.	If prototypes were developed using computer-assisted design, they could be transmitted to the team by desktop videoconferencing, access from the intranet, and even shown as holographic projections in the meeting room.
The team could request a preliminary go-ahead on a project idea from management.	The team could prepare a short video presentation or slide show that would be transmitted to management (worldwide, if need be) for review prior to a meeting via meeting room teleconferencing.

being fired from a computer company where they both worked, as part of corporate downsizing. She then informed him that she was taking a job in Paris, France, but that they could maintain a "virtual" relationship via the Internet. The horror on Doonesbury's face clearly communicated that he did not believe it would be an equivalent experience.

This raises the key question: How many senses does it take for an effective communication? Doonesbury clearly be-

Figure 10. Orbits of participation for particular meetings.

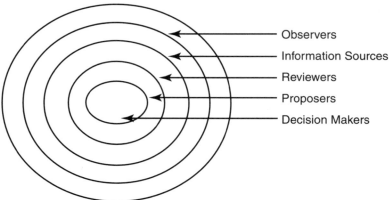

Observers

Information Sources

Reviewers

Proposers

Decision Makers

lieved that touch was a necessary part of his relationship with his girlfriend (and if researchers into pheromones are right, so is the sense of smell).

In our opinion, to build trust or resolve conflicts people need the full sensory information that comes only from in-person interaction. Trust is built on knowing the other person, and knowing seems to involve all five senses, and maybe even some senses that science does not acknowledge.

But not every meeting transaction requires the same number of senses. If you simply need to confirm that a task has been completed, e-mail may do just fine. If you need to get agreement on the seating arrangements for an upcoming con-ference, you would do better to use a technology that permits everybody to see a picture. Similarly, if you want people to see how a large number of tasks interrelate to achieve a goal, it helps if everybody can see these tasks displayed not just on paper but on the wall or another large space. If you want to get agreement on the design of a new product, you may find it extremely useful if people can see it modeled, or even as a 3-D hologram. People can be far more comfortable with the design of a new facility if they can simulate the experience of walking around inside it. Certain ceremonial events—unveil-ing a new product—require all the pizzazz of multimedia sound, color, action. Different types of meetings require more senses. You may even want to ask yourself the question, How many senses will it take for this meeting to be a success? This will help match the technology to the meeting purpose.

Match the Technology, Process, and Facility to the Type of Meeting

Meetings that use the innovations described in this book are most likely to be effective when there is a synergy among the type of meeting, the technology used, the meeting processes used, and the meeting facility. Below are our personal observations about the critical considerations for each type of meeting, as well as suggestions for which type of technology, process, and facility may be most appropriate for each type. Remember that some meetings are clearly a hybrid; that is, one item to be covered involves one meeting purpose, e.g., it's a decision-making item, while the next involves another purpose, e.g., it's an informational item. Hybrid meetings may require changing the technology to match each change in the meeting agenda.

Information Briefings

Information briefings are prime candidates for electronic technology. Many current meetings could be eliminated or shortened by the use of e-mail or the intranet. People could then get the information whenever they wanted it, from wherever they are.

This assumes, however, that the source of the information is credible. In other words, once trust has been built, then people may be fully satisfied with electronic communication. If there is no prior relationship, if communication is strained by past history, or if people believe the information is self-serving, then electronic communication may not be enough. It's not enough to consider the medium of communication; you also have to consider the source.

It's also necessary to consider whether the purpose of

giving the information is simply to inform, to engage, or to motivate. If the other person simply needs a piece of information and is motivated to use it, then the simplest forms of electronic communication may be the best way to go. If you want the other person to come to grips emotionally with an issue, you may need to engage more senses (by using more sophisticated technology). People also retain material better if they interact with it. If you really want people to walk away with the information, one-way communication may not be the best approach. Finally, if you want behavioral change, the more senses are involved, and the more interactive the communication, the more likely that change is going to be.

E-mail is great for simple information exchange. An organizational intranet provides an extremely valuable tool for information exchange and could eliminate the need for many information-only meetings. Intranet allows multimedia communication, and allows people to seek out the information that is directly useful. Intranet also allows people to respond by completing a form or making comments. If credibility or engagement is an issue, videoconferencing is preferable, providing more sensory information and the opportunity for direct interaction.

Truly effective use of an intranet assumes a democratization of access to information. In organizations where access to information is a form of status or power, intranet may be a waste or may even breed cynicism. Also, intranet requires someone to coordinate, coach, or prod the sharing of information. Totally voluntary sharing of information often trips over the fact that it takes time and resources to make information available to other people in a form they can use.

For most simple information exchange, it's not necessary to use sophisticated group processes; nor is a facilitator needed. But if you wish to engage people, or stimulate interaction, use structured exercises in which people "try out" the concept, then comment on it based on that experience.

Many information briefings can be better handled in the desktop environment than by gathering people in a room. There is little benefit to bringing people together unless you want interaction, either questions and answers (which could also be handled via intranet), or some activity where people are asked to apply the information.

Trust Building/Team Building

In our experience, relationship or trust building is best accomplished in face-to-face interaction. We do not believe that electronic participation should be substituted for face-to-face participation for trust building or team building unless there is little alternative. On the other hand, various electronic technologies—access to databases, electronic process charts, modeling and simulation—might be used to support the meeting. The meeting itself might be held in an interactive meeting space or alternatively in an informal setting away from offices and competing demands.

Since trust requires knowing the person, there is a heightened need in this type of meeting for informal social activities, or structured group activities where participants share more about themselves than they might normally in a business setting. A wide variety of team building techniques are available. This is the kind of session where a facilitator might be valuable both in designing and conducting the session, although some structure for team discussions can be provided by using group graphics/process templates.

Since trust building/team building requires getting to know people as people, not just as organizational role players, the meeting should be in a setting away from the office, in a place where the cues that keep people acting their roles are scarce. If it's a task-oriented team building session, an interactive meeting center would be ideal. If the meeting is more oriented toward trust building, a retreat setting may be more appropriate.

In many organizations the need for relationship or trust building is rarely acknowledged explicitly. However, these organizations may sponsor golf matches or other social events that are really designed to accomplish a similar purpose. Such events do have value, but in many cases a well-designed team building session, with accompanying social events, will accomplish far more.

Decision-Making Meetings

Typically, a decision-making meeting is a culmination of a number of prior meetings. The problem has already been defined, options have been generated and evaluated, and now it is time to make a choice.

The meeting format may vary depending on whether all the people at the table (whether a wooden table or an electronic table) are participants in making the decision—as they might be in participatory decision making—or if most are there to provide information or bear witness while one or a few leaders make the decision.

A key impediment to designing effective decision-making meetings is the failure to include the appropriate people in the decision-making or -implementing process. Nothing is more frustrating than building a high level of team commitment to a decision only to discover that the people who arrived at that decision do not have the authority to implement it, or that the people who are essential for implementation were not even invited. Particularly if the decision is to be made in a participatory manner, or if the decision commits multiple organizational units without any one person being able to make the decision, it's imperative that there be careful analysis of who needs to be in the room (real or electronic) for the decision to count.

There are various ranking processes that may help people in arriving at a decision, but while such processes help clarify the issues they can't make the decision for anyone.

If the decision makers are a group of equals, or if the decision maker wishes to participate in the discussion, a facilitator may be useful. Much of the "information providing" could be readily handled by videoconference, and in some cases by prerecorded multimedia presentations (with the presenter available by videoconference in case the decision makers have questions).

There is value to having subordinates observe a decision being made so they understand the basis for that decision. Much of this function could be handled by videotape. The entire meeting could be recorded on video, with the entire tape or key portions available on the intranet for anyone who is interested.

Decisions may be facilitated by having instant access to databases, or being able to draw on information from the intranet. Ideally this information would then be projected onto the wall, so that all participants have access to the information.

Selection of the facility will be driven by two issues: the number of people who need to be physically present, and the amount of electronic support required. Generally speaking, decision making goes best in a smaller, intimate setting. But this may be counterbalanced by the need to have staff present, or to use a room that provides the full array of electronic support.

Decision-making meetings are often as much about power and status as they are about what is good for the organization. It's not unusual for a key executive to bring a large entourage to a meeting, not because they are needed but to exhibit the person's power, and to reinforce the perception among meeting participants of the executive's status. Technology will not solve this problem. Similarly, subordinates sometimes are eager to be included in such meetings, even if they do not participate in decision making, because of the status they derive from being invited.

Do not assume that because someone is participating via videoconference that he/she is at a competitive disadvantage with those present in the room. Often, more conversations are directed at the person on the screen than at people physically present.

Program/Project Planning or Review

Program/project planning meetings benefit greatly from the use of group process and electronic technologies. Critical considerations include: helping the participants visualize how all the tasks fit together; providing useful access to data about task completion, expenditure of time, and allocation of staff; and including all key stakeholders in the meeting. (This assumes that managers *want* team members to have access to data about task completion, staff allocation, and resource expenditures. If that information is tightly held by managers, there is little value in electronic access.)

Because project meetings are a mix of briefings, problem solving, and decision making, all key participants need to be there, physically or virtually. In order to get the full benefit of a project meeting, there must be careful prior analysis of who the stakeholders are, so they will be included. Research shows a tendency to leave key people or groups out, with their exclusion invariably becoming an impediment.

Assuming reasonable trust and no major conflicts in the group, participation can be by videoconferencing. Teleconferencing (either desktop or meeting room) is less effective because participants cannot visualize the process or project. Minutes of the meeting, or even video clips, can be available on intranet bulletin boards for anybody who is interested.

Project meetings cry out for the ability to display whole projects and processes on the wall and to manipulate the elements and edit the process. Some form of visual group memory is essential. Participants can then see their progress and understand the interconnections. Facilitation can be very helpful.

Project meetings require a room where participants can work on the walls. A room at an interactive meeting center may be particularly appropriate for this type of meeting. If people are going to participate by videoconferencing, it may be important to have a room with a large screen so that video participants appear near normal size to participants in the meeting room.

Dispute Resolution Meetings

As organizations get flatter, they will need to become even more skilled at resolving disputes, because they will not be able to rely on the boss to resolve issues quickly. Organizations that leave issues unresolved will not have the agility to meet customers' needs in a timely manner. So the dispute resolution meeting will become much more common.

If the dispute is personal, or involves power struggles within the organization, face-to-face interaction is recommended. Disputes about substantive issues, such as money, time, or staff, are actually not as difficult to resolve as disputes about relationships, power, status, or control (although these are often mixed in with disputes about substantive issues). Disputes based on different knowledge or uneven access to factual information may be particularly suited to resolution using electronic access to data.

People often need to state their differences strongly before they can begin to build upon shared interests. Skilled facilitators help structure activities to ensure that these feelings are expressed, but in a way that permits productive resolution. Use of dispute resolution approaches such as interest-based negotiation may also help resolve disputes. When disputes are bitter, use of a third-party neutral such as a mediator may be helpful. Participating in partnering workshops at the front end of a project may help prevent disputes.

People have trouble letting go of feelings or positions until they feel understood. Facilitators often record comments or concerns on flip charts, whiteboards, or walls so that people can actually see their concern was acknowledged.

A primary use of electronic technologies will be to give everybody equal access to information. Dissenting viewpoints can be presented directly to decision makers via video- or teleconferencing, so that people are confident their concerns have been well represented at dispute resolution meetings.

Privacy and noise isolation are critical considerations. If people are going to resolve disputes they need to be able to express themselves without fear of being overheard, or worrying about raised voices. It's also essential that the meeting be free of interruptions, and that the participants can keep the room as long as they need it—you do not want an issue to go unresolved because at a critical juncture the janitor has to clean the room or the building is being locked up.

Generating New Ideas or Approaches

New ideas can come from anywhere in the organization. So technologies that make it easy to gather and display comments from throughout the organization may open up new ways of approaching problems. Anyone in the organization can submit ideas by intranet. The problem can be posted on an intranet home page, and graphics or even videos can be attached to text.

But in order for brainstorming to have value, it's imperative that the problem be well defined. A "generating ideas" meeting (or electronic "all-comers" session) should not be the first meeting in the series, but should follow a problem-definition meeting that clarifies the issues, defines the interests that have to be met, and specifies what constitutes success.

There are advantages to using techniques that make ideas anonymous, that is, ensuring that they are not associated with people or groups that can be perceived as trying to aggrandize their own position. Ideas submitted by intranet can be anonymous, and even if everyone is in the same room, ideas can be submitted anonymously if participants have a keyboard or slate and there is appropriate groupware.

Techniques such as brainstorming or nominal group process have proven to be superior to mixing idea generation and evaluation. There are numerous other techniques and exercises that can be used to stimulate creative thinking, and research shows that a combination of lots of stimulus and a playful atmosphere increases creativity.

"Working big" on a wall or whiteboard helps people think more creatively and builds group involvement. Interactive meeting centers are ideal for idea generation, with a core group in the meeting center, and other people connected electronically. The use of computer models or simulations can help people understand systems or whole processes, helping them visualize possible solutions.

Inviting widespread participation may create an aura of participation that does not reflect reality in many organizations. As a minimum, reciprocity requires that when people are invited to participate, they should be given feedback on how their ideas were used. If people feel it was just an exercise and their ideas were not taken seriously, their participation will drop off very rapidly. This means that time must be spent acknowledging comments and giving people some idea of why and how ideas were used.

Strategic Planning

This type of meeting typically involves a full day or more of intense interaction. These are often data-rich meetings, with the need for people to prepare carefully prior to the meeting and to have full access to data during the meeting. Since strategic planning sessions occur infrequently and commit valuable management resources for a concentrated period of time, it is essential that the participants have all the support they need—logistic and electronic—to ensure completion.

A strategic planning session is valuable only when management has sufficient information about the organization and the external environment. If management is out of touch, the decisions it reaches in strategic planning sessions may seem unreal to staff or customers. There is a need for a "sensing" process prior to a strategic planning session, so that both problems and ideas can bubble up (from staff) or bubble in (from suppliers or customers) before the session begins. This type of meeting requires the full involvement of the senior leader. There is nothing more frustrating than going through this kind of session, reaching a conclusion, then having it overruled by someone who was not even in on the discussion.

This is a work-to-the-walls type of meeting. After all, the organization is trying to "see" where it is going, and this needs the support of full graphic displays and process guides. This is also the type of meeting where it is important to have full data access, and the ability to display the data for the group (either by printing them out, or preferably, by projecting them onto the wall). Facilitation is particularly valuable for this kind of meeting, both in designing and conducting the meeting. The meeting will also be aided by using graphic process guides that help people visualize where the organization has been and where it is going.

This type of meeting works very well in an interactive meeting center with full group process and electronic support, as well as logistics staff available as needed. A retreat setting can be useful for getting people out of their normal roles, but only if adequate support is available and the group can work on the walls.

Problem-Solving Sessions

Problem-solving sessions are often time driven in response to
an immediate crisis. The most effective solution is to have all
key actors physically present, so a solution can be found and
an implementation plan developed before people leave the
room. But often people are scattered all over when the crisis
arises, so electronic participation will be necessary. The more
electronically supported senses that can be included, the
better.

Because people are under pressure this can be an "everybody talking all at once" kind of meeting, with the danger of
disputes arising. Although there may not be time to obtain a
facilitator, the leader or a designee may still want to act as a
facilitator to handle the intense interaction. Because of the
sense of urgency it is particularly important to acknowledge
people's concerns by recording them visually (this reduces the
emotional pressure). Be certain that the discussion comes to
a clear resolution. There can be a tendency to rush back to fire
fighting just when there is some sense of direction and just a
few minutes before there is complete clarification of the action
plan.

While videoconferencing would be a good technology for
problem-solving sessions, such sessions often take place under
time pressures that mean that some people are participating
by phone, others at desktops, others on meeting room videoconferences. Problem-solving sessions are a natural for desktop videoconferencing, because people can participate at the
nearest desktop computer and can access their own files
through the intranet.

The best problem solving occurs when the key actors can
be brought in immediately, either physically or electronically,
regardless of where they are located in the organization chart.
If everybody has to go through channels, the crisis may have
swamped the organization before all the approvals are obtained. Electronic communication will make it easier to let
everybody—including bosses of participants—know what is
happening.

Building Commitment

This is the type of meeting where management needs to build commitment or support for the organization to go in a new direction, or reorganize or refocus. Typically the concerns of the organization are treated as paramount, and the concerns of employees are treated as secondary details to be addressed later. As a result, it is actually the type of meeting most likely to build cynicism among employees.

Think through what employee concerns may be before you go public with your announcement. Remember that people's first reaction will be based on "How does this affect me?" Also, employees are watching to see management's commitment to the new approach. If management just makes a single electronic announcement regarding a major decision, this will be read as either "they don't really support this," or "they don't care about its impact on us peons."

One of the key principles of group process is "commitment is built through participation and interaction." This is the type of meeting where one-way communication alone can be deadly. This is an opportunity for management to use electronic media to communicate directly with employees.

Make your presentations "local"—use videoconferencing to have a series of short electronic sessions with each key organizational unit, so they feel they communicated with you personally on this important issue. Create an electronic mechanism so everybody can see what everybody else is saying and thinking. Use the intranet or desktop videoconferencing as a way employees can communicate back to management. Design this so some forms of communication are anonymous but shared with everyone, so that you know how people are really reacting.

Management needs to be present in a room that permits all forms of electronic interaction. Avoid rooms that emphasize the majesty of office. This is a time to emphasize "we're all in this together," not the all-too-apparent separation of senior management from the rest of the organization.

Celebrations

Every organization needs occasional celebrations when sales figures are up, customer satisfaction is higher, a new product is announced, or employees are being honored for successful performance.

In celebrations, the emphasis needs to be on "us"—"we did it." Celebrations need to be about the whole organization, not about management. If you are going to emphasize teams, then recognition needs to be given to teams, not just individuals. This kind of celebration can breed cynicism or isolation if people or groups feel left out.

In smaller organizations, celebrations are best done by gathering everybody together. If people are going to gather in a single large room, get the furniture out of the way so that people can talk and relate to each other comfortably. Use color, lights, music.

In larger organizations this is not possible, so the idea is to use electronic media to create a "virtual" version of being all together. Everybody can have some involvement electronically, even if they cannot be physically present. Flash a message on the intranet desktop that an important announcement is coming. Use the full panoply of graphics and sound to make the event seem important. Use electronic media to appeal to the senses. Make it fun and stimulating.

Informal ("in the Hallway") Meetings

Particularly among knowledge workers, informal interaction is an important way that ideas get spread across organizational lines. These are, by nature, unstructured happenings. The key issue is whether the organization supports these kinds of interactions. This is both a cultural issue—do people feel approval or disapproval for informal interactions?—and a facility issue—does the facility provide appropriate spaces for informal interaction?

If the organizational culture frowns on socializing, efforts to construct facilities that encourage socializing are probably meaningless. At the same time, the organizational culture should encourage the kind of socializing where people talk about ideas and work, not just personal issues.

Spaces where people pass each other, such as hallways or stairways, should be designed so people feel comfortable to pull off to the side and talk. Provide small informal spaces with coffee and tea on the boundaries between organizations, so that people are encouraged to talk informally with those in other parts of the organization. Design cafeterias or other social spaces as if they were intended to support productivity, rather than to be isolated from the work experience. Provide whiteboards or other means by which ideas can be recorded. Provide support to the intranet throughout the building. This provides access to databases and to individual files.

Minimize Awareness of the Technology

Despite the emphasis on technology throughout the book, remember this important caveat: If people have to think too much about running the technology, they will not be concentrating on the task at hand. And, on the other hand, even if they are enthralled by the technology, they may be thinking about it, not the problem. The challenge of introducing collaborative technologies is to make it sufficiently intuitive that it does not require significant relearning. Make the technology act and feel as much as possible like technology people use every day. If learning is required, there must be sufficient training so that using the equipment has become habitual, rather than something requiring conscious effort. If the technology is powerful but complicated, provide staffing and support so the users get the power without having to master unfamiliar technology.

Note

1. Personal interview with Bob Hoss, Worldwide Director of Telecommunications, IBM Corporation, September 9, 1996.

9

Developing a Business Rationale for Collaborative Technology

It's easy to grasp the promise of collaborative technologies. Among the obvious virtues of an approach combining collaborative technologies and group process innovations are:

○ People can participate from anywhere in the world, so long as they are connected via phone or satellite.
○ People can participate anytime, whenever it is convenient for them.
○ It's convenient and easy to share information with anyone who may want or need it—in case you forget someone, just put it on the electronic bulletin board that other employees can pick up worldwide.
○ People can participate at the level they want, drawing on as much information or as little as they need.
○ Remote communication is not just limited to words. People can communicate with images, models, and simulations. The technology can provide information in multiple senses, increasing the experience of actually being there.
○ Issues can be resolved quickly before they cause delays or hard feelings.
○ Team leaders can use targeted group processes to stim-

ulate creativity, speed up evaluation, or resolve conflicts.
○ It will be far easier to access specialized expertise, without all the attendant costs.

The payoffs should be:

○ More commitment to decisions that have been reached
○ Quicker resolution—faster time to market
○ More creativity
○ Involvement of more people without slowing down
the process
○ More access to data at the point of decision
○ More efficient use of time
○ More expertise to bear on the problem

There is hard evidence that such payoffs are possible and
not just the wishful thinking of devotees:

○ A 1987 study at IBM showed that meeting time was
cut 56% by the use of groupware.[1]
○ Although Apple Computer spent $6 million on video-
conferencing hardware, software, training and staffing, it estimated savings of $28 million in a very short
time. It was not cheap, but it was cost-effective.[2]
○ Boeing conducted a study of the use of groupware in
64 meetings with 1,000 participants. It estimated an
average savings of $6,700 per meeting (a total savings
of $428,000).[3]
○ Silicon Graphics estimates a 95% cost reduction in getting information disseminated internally through use
of an intranet web site. In particular, it found a document control team now took only 30 minutes to obtain
complete information about a part, as compared with
a prior 20-hour average.[4]

Obtaining payoffs such as these will be essential in the
future. The *San Jose Mercury* reports that the number one cate-
gory of capital spending by U.S. companies since 1990 is com-

puters and communications gear. Companies that can get
more return on this investment will have a significant competitive advantage.[5]

Organizational Issues Make a Big Difference

Achieving these gains is not automatic. Organizational issues
can completely mask some of these savings. Boeing, despite
its reported savings of $6,700 per meeting, has dropped its
use of groupware. An article in *Fortune* magazine reports that
Boeing is not talking about why it dropped groupware, but
the author of the article speculates that old-style managers
were uncomfortable about being placed in the spotlight by
groupware, even if the technology made for faster decisions.[6]
    As discussed in Chapter Four, a study of the use of collab-
orative technology at 3-M, Varian, and an unnamed high-tech
manufacturer revealed that the technology itself was secondary as a constraint on use of the technology. That is not to say
that there were not technical issues, but people figured out
how to work around them.
    The big problems turned out to be:

○ People in the organizations often didn't know why
  they should collaborate.
○ There were organizational disincentives for collaborating in situations where rewards were based on individual or functional performance.
○ When there were prior organizational conflicts, people
  just wouldn't talk to each other.

Organizations have immune systems not unlike the
human body. Every step in introducing a new approach or
technology may come in conflict with the habits and technology that already exist. There are winners and losers, even if
unintended.

Innovation and Productivity

During the 1984 Superbowl, Apple Computer ran an advertisement featuring a runner who ran up the aisle between rows of dronelike workers obediently listening to the pronouncements of a Big Brother–like figure and threw a hammer that shattered the screen showing Big Brother's larger-than-life image. The ad was clearly a slap at IBM, which at the time dominated the computer world. It was also a challenge to mainframe computing, the world of the sterile-air centralized computer presided over by the white-coated information management acolytes. The founders of Apple clearly recognized that the PC (particularly their Macintosh) put computing power in the hands of the people. It was a way of breaking the stranglehold of the Establishment and defying the representatives of authority.

Today, Apple is struggling, and some fear it will fade into a footnote in history. IBM is hardly the all-powerful controlling enterprise it once was. If the ad was run today, the bully would probably be Bill Gates and the marketing mavens at Microsoft.

Apple got one thing right, though. The personal computer, whichever brand, did put tremendous computing power in the hands of individuals. And it did mean that computing power was no longer the province of a few within the organization.

But then a funny thing happened: People wanted to connect. It may well prove that the greatest virtue of the PC is not to distribute raw computing power throughout the organization—although it certainly does that—but to connect with other people, information, and tools. Anyone with a PC, a modem, and a phone line (or satellite link) can access a whole universe of information, make connections worldwide to other people with shared interests, and communicate his/her needs, problems, and services to virtually anyone on earth. The real payoff of the new technology is connectivity. All those little pockets of information scattered throughout the organization, or throughout the world, are now available to virtually any individual.

Ever since the introduction of the computer into organizational life, there have been cynics who pointed out that all the promises of dramatic increases in productivity based on the investment in computer hardware are not borne out by the figures. During the 1970s and 1980s, the era of the mainframes, nonfarm business productivity was in the doldrums.

The introduction of the PC was supposed to change all that. Yet, until recently, it was hard to point to large across-the-board increases that could be attributed to investment in PCs. When interviewed in 1992, Bill Gates argued that productivity gains were there; they were just difficult to measure.[7] Jim Manzi of Lotus, who was just in the process of introducing Lotus Notes, the first large-scale groupware product, was more candid in admitting that it was hard to find evidence of productivity increases from stand-alone computers. He argued, however, that the payoff would come as all those stand-alone computers were connected to permit collaborative work and access to information.[8]

Manzi may have been right. Research shows that productivity has begun to rise significantly in the early 1990s. Erik Bryjolfsson, an MIT economist who conducted many of these recent studies, concludes that: "Information technology, as of 1994, is one of the big contributors to growth."[9] Bill Gates is convinced. He has recently committed Microsoft to a strategy that places huge emphasis on products to connect computers via the Internet.

The idea that it has taken all this time to figure out how to get the payoff from the technology is not inconsistent with the history of other major technological innovations. This history shows that it may take decades for organizations to reconceptualize processes to take advantage of the innovation.

Architect Frank Lloyd Wright observed that humankind started out making shelters with sticks and stones. Eventually we developed tools that allowed us to cut logs. This created new structural possibilities. But, Wright observed, we built log buildings as if we were building with sticks and stones. When steel came along, he argued, we built buildings as if they were built of logs. When prestressed concrete was developed, we built as if with steel. It simply takes time to understand the possibilities in the new technologies and stop impos-ing the limitations and constraints of how we worked in the past.[10]

Paul David, a Stanford economist who studied the intro-duction of electricity into manufacturing, draws a similar con-clusion. He reports: "When electricity was first introduced, captains of industry did nothing more than unhook their steam engines or water wheels and replace them with electric dynamos. From the point of view of the internal organization of the factory, nothing changed." But over time, he states, manufacturers began to figure out how to harness the benefits of electricity. Improvements in electric motor technology al-lowed manufacturers to use electricity more flexibly, and man-ufacturing processes were altered to take advantage of elec-tricity.

From the 1890s, manufacturing productivity climbed at a modest 0.3%–0.5% annual growth rate. Then, in the 1920s, productivity exploded. Professor David attributes at least three quarters of that growth to electrification. "That was the fulfillment of the dynamo," he says, "but it took the reengi-neering and reconceptualization of manufacturing for it to happen." David concludes that "there is a co-evolution of the technology and the organizational structure, which is likely in the early stages to require a lot of experimentation and learning."[11]

This analogy may fit well with information technology. A number of people have reported that among the barriers to increased productivity from the use of information technology are:

○ Organizations keep the old systems operating along-side the new systems, "just in case." In many cases, the backup system is never eliminated, and the new system is force-fitted to conform to the old one.
○ The technology is often used inefficiently. This may be due to the need for training (it's clear that one of the virtues of PCs is that they take a lot less time to learn how to operate than a mainframe), and the need to overcome resistance based on old habits (which is why

we have to ask our children to show us how to program our VCRs).
○ Information technology is introduced piecemeal,
rather than as an integrated approach.
○ Managers are still holding on to information, because
information is power.

These are important considerations for one simple reason—organizations cannot introduce collaborative meeting
technologies on a completely piecemeal basis. If people
wanted to find out what a PC could do, they could buy one
and try it. But if you want to find out how desktop videoconferencing works, you have to have a critical mass of people
with the right equipment before it becomes natural and normal for people to communicate that way. To make it truly
effective it has to be tied into local area networks, and it should
even be built into the desktop that people see when they boot
up their machines. Until there is this level of comfort and integration, you will not know with assurance just how big the
payoff will be.

Motivations for Introducing Meeting Technologies

Two motivations for introducing collaborative technologies
relate to the bottom line, but clearly go far beyond cost-benefit
analysis:

Setting the Pace

Everyone dreams of being the industry leader, the pace setter.
Some organizations have made being the leader part of the
organizational culture, so that early adoption of new and better technologies is consistently encouraged and supported.
Madison Square Garden has the goal of being the technology
leader among arenas, an appropriate goal for "the World's
Most Famous Arena." Not every organization can afford to
do this, and some that have lived on the cutting edge of tech-

nology have also died by it. "Second-generation" technology is sometimes more user-friendly and better integrated with existing technology. Early adopters need to be willing to absorb some false starts and reworking in order to maintain their leadership role.

Keeping Pace With the Competition

In this age of worldwide competition, the fear of falling behind the competition provides a constant incentive to change. This fear can be based on a realistic assessment of the situation, or it can be simply based on an "if we do not have one, and the other guys do, we'll look bad" reaction. A strategy based on paranoia, as Intel's Andrew Grove describes it, can be very effective. But it can be dangerous if it labels the organization as always a step behind and crashing to catch up.

The total quality improvement movement introduced the concept of benchmarking, in which organizations measure themselves against their competitors. Certainly if a competitor is a step ahead in technology, and that has led to improved market share or profitability, this is a powerful argument for your organization to catch up. But one of the first steps of benchmarking is a careful analysis of those areas in which a comparison between you and your competitors makes a difference to your success. There is no reason to use technology just because the other guy did, unless that technology is making an important contribution to the other guy's success.

Developing a Business Rationale for Collaborative Technology

Cost-benefit analysis is a cornerstone for most successful businesses. Yet Jim Adams's own recent experience developing a business rationale for collaborative technology at Madison Square Garden is a reminder of how frustrating it is trying to force-fit the amount of organizational change implied by collaborative technologies into a neat cost-benefit analysis.

The desire to be the leader or the fear of falling behind can motivate significant organizational change that is based on more than a cost-benefit analysis. The very nature of maintaining leadership in innovation is to make decisions at precisely those times when there is not a basis in experience for either the cost or benefit side of the formula.

One of the challenges in estimating costs and benefits is that determining which costs or benefits matter depends on where you sit in the organization. Middle management—people who are evaluated based on whether a project is on time, in budget—is worried about the more tangible benefits of collaborative work, such as reduced travel time and cost. But the kinds of benefits in which senior management is interested are precisely the benefits that are softer and harder to quantify—quicker decisions, broader participation, improved decision making, and reduced process time.

Despite the difficulties in forcing major innovations into the cost-benefit model, and despite the difficulties in quantifying exactly those benefits that are probably the best reasons for the innovation, we still believe that a serious business rationale needs to be developed. We believe that a well-developed business rationale is an important precursor of an effective implementation strategy. It is always harder to do a good job if you do not know why you are doing it.

Here are some of the questions we believe need to be answered to develop that rationale:

1. *What is the problem or need that makes you consider collaborative technology?* What is the problem you think you are solving, e.g., time to market, cross-functional collaboration, or access to information? Where in the organization is this need located? What will solving this problem or addressing this need do for the organization? Make sure you are not starting with a solution, then looking for a problem it can solve.

2. *Why now?* Identify any drivers that create a sense of urgency. Are there any time constraints or reasons it has to be completed by a particular time?

3. *How will collaborative technology satisfy these needs?* First,

carefully consider all alternatives to be sure whether collaborative technology is the best solution to the problem or the best means to meet the needs. If not, consider adopting the other solutions. If you are satisfied that collaborative technology is the best answer, develop a clear statement of why it is the solution, and describe how it will address the problem.

4. *Which collaborative innovations are appropriate for your organization?* The answers to this question may include the need for changes in corporate culture, or innovations in meeting processes, meeting technology, or meeting facilities. These changes are most effective when all of these elements are addressed simultaneously, and when the implementation plan uses each of the changes to reinforce the others.

5. *How will the collaborative technology interface with existing systems?* Your organization already has a significant investment in information technology. How will new technologies interface with the existing system? The ideal solution is one where the new meeting technology looks and feels like the rest of the technology the organization uses. Does this require adaptation of the collaborative technology to your existing technology, or is it time to update the look and feel of the entire system? Your organization already has meeting facilities. Will the innovations require changes in existing facilities? Will new facilities be needed? How will the ways the organization presently plans meetings need to be changed? What training will be needed? What changes in policies and procedures may be required?

6. *What is the value of solving the problem or satisfying this need?* How important is it that this problem be solved or need addressed? Even if you cannot quantify the cost-benefit ratio of the innovation, can you demonstrate that solving this problem or developing this new competency addresses an issue that is so central to your organization's well-being that it justifies the time, effort, and resources that it will take? Keep in mind that "value" is not always in dollars and cents. If the proposed innovations do not address a problem that is central to your organization's future, you are going to have a tough sell.

7. *What is the cost (direct, indirect, operating, and mainte-nance) of the innovation?* Table 5 lists some of the costs you may want to consider.

8. *What are the benefits?* Not all the benefits are quantifi-able, but do the best you can to assign a value to those benefits you can measure. Then explain in writing why you believe the innovations will result in the "softer" benefits. Table 6 provides some checklists.

In the course of preparing a business rationale you will identify a number of implementation issues that are important for your action plan. You may also recognize the need to define appropriate measurements ("metrics") of effective meetings. But in our experience, unless management is convinced that there is a significant problem these innovations address, or that these innovations are likely to address a core issue for the organization, the numbers alone will not be sufficient. But in the process you will learn a great deal that will help you with implementation.

Notes

1. David Kirkpatrick, "Here Comes the Payoffs From PCS," *Fortune,* March 23, 1992, pp. 93–99.
2. Andrew Kupfer, "Prime Time for Videoconferences," *For-tune,* December 28, 1992.
3. Kirkpatrick, op. cit.
4. STRATIQUEST, "The Benefits of Collaborative Comput-ing: An Independent Multi-Company Study," 1996. Avail-able from Stratiquest, 353 Rancho Rio Road, Ben Lomand, Calif. 95005-9477.
5. *San Jose Mercury,* March 2, 1997.
6. David Kirkpatrick, "Groupware Goes Boom," *Fortune,* De-cember 27, 1993, pp. 99–103.
7. Kirkpatrick, 1992, op. cit.
8. Kirkpatrick, ibid.
9. Myron Magnet, "The Productivity Payoff Arrives," *For-tune,* June 27, 1994.

(Text continues on page 145)

Table 5. Costs of collaboration innovations.

Meeting Technology Costs	Meeting Process Costs	Meeting Facilities Costs
Hardware	*Training Costs*	*Physical Facilities*
○ Projectors, computers, wall displays, whiteboards, televisions, videoconferencing equipment (desktop and meeting room)	○ Training in meeting leadership, facilitation, visual group recording, use of process software, including: —Trainers —Training materials —Training facility —Staff time spent in training —Travel	○ New interactive meeting facilities (total facility cost) ○ Retrofitting wiring, phone lines, and electrical devices for new equipment ○ Physical space for teams and for informal conversations
Software		*Furniture, Equipment*
○ Groupware (joint tasking, presentation, modeling, simulation) ○ Individual productivity applications (e.g., word processing, spreadsheets) ○ System software enabling networks, conferencing, and collaboration	*Facilitators/Process Design Consultants* ○ External consultants ○ Consultant travel ○ Hiring/training of internal facilitators ○ Staff time spent facilitating meetings not directly tied to their job	○ Movable walls and furniture ○ Mounted whiteboards or other visual recording devices on walls *Staffing* ○ Increased maintenance due to use of walls ○ Logistics support for meeting centers/skunkworks

(Continues)

Table 5. *(Continued)*

Meeting Technology Costs	Meeting Process Costs	Meeting Facilities Costs
Support Staff	*Productivity Losses*	
○ Technicians/support staff to install the technology and get it operating in an integrated manner	○ Time spent learning new processes	
	○ Increased time spent in meeting planning	
○ Technicians/support staff to help operate the meeting technologies	○ Time spent in meetings talking about process	
○ Technicians to maintain the meeting technologies	*Group Process Software*	
Transaction Charges		
○ Line charges, including initial, periodic, and per transaction, for data network, telecommunications, and television		
○ Service fees for third-party services to facilitate individual transactions (including accounting, billing, and connecting)		

Meeting Technology Costs	Meeting Process Costs	Meeting Facilities Costs
Operations		
○ Training to use the technology		
○ Supplies		
○ Lost productivity for planning the transition, and during the change from the old to the new		
○ Consultants used to assist and audit, both during the transition and during ongoing operations		
○ Shutdowns of computers, electric service, and network during conversion		

Table 6. Benefits of collaboration innovations.

Meeting Technology Benefits	Meeting Process Benefits	Meeting Facilities Benefits
Quantifiable Benefits	*Quantifiable Benefits*	*Quantifiable Benefits*
Reduced Travel Costs	○ Reduced number of meetings on the same topic	○ Greater satisfaction with meeting space
○ Intraorganizational meetings	○ Less time spent in each meeting/less time on each agenda item	○ Increased use of interactive meeting rooms in comparison to conventional meeting rooms
○ Meetings with customers		
Reduced Travel Time	○ Greater satisfaction with meetings	○ Greater interaction/higher levels of participation
○ Lost productivity—time in transit to other places	○ Decision or agreement resolved the issue or defined the course of action	○ Increased business-related socialization, e.g., serendipitous informal meetings
○ Lost productivity—time within the office complex	○ Disputes resolved through mutual agreements	
Reduced Consultant Costs		○ Increased work efficiency of project teams
○ Reduced travel costs		
○ Payment only for time used		
○ Timely availability		

Meeting Technology Benefits	Meeting Process Benefits	Meeting Facilities Benefits
"Softer" Benefits	*"Softer" Benefits*	*"Softer" Benefits*
○ Broader participation	○ Broader participation	○ Greater creativity
○ Accelerated decision making—reduced process time	○ Better decisions	○ Improved ability of participants to visualize problems or processes
○ Improved access to information/better-quality decisions	○ Increased creativity	○ Improved productivity
	○ Improved coordination/cooperation between organizational units	○ Enhanced team identity
○ Improved intercompany communication flow	○ More commitment to the decisions made in meetings—decisions made in meetings lead to implementation	○ Improved cross-organizational communication
○ Improved employee quality of life (reduced travel hassle, more time with families)	○ Less need to get subsequent reviews/sign-offs	
○ Improved customer service—more contact with customers	○ Accelerated decision making	
○ Faster time-to-market—including electronic reviews, participation of all key organizational elements during the decision		

(Continues)

Table 6. *(Continued)*

Meeting Technology Benefits	Meeting Process Benefits	Meeting Facilities Benefits
"Softer" Benefits		
○ Leveraging of internal experts—internal experts can be accessed from many locations simultaneously		
○ Emergency response capability		
○ Reduced mistakes because all parties are looking at the same picture		
○ Reduced documentation time		

10. Jim Creighton distinctly remembers reading this observation by Frank Lloyd Wright more than 30 years ago. Unfortunately, a diligent search has not turned up the reference. But the quote so impressed Creighton that he's been thinking about it ever since, and he's sure the quote is out there—somewhere.
11. Magnet, op. cit.

10

Introducing Collaborative Technology in Large Organizations

Creating an effective collaboration system in your organization is not just an issue of technology. It will involve group process innovation, technology deployment, and facility reconfiguration. It will also involve careful planning to ensure that you develop a program that fits your current corporate culture or recognizes that changing the corporate culture is an essential accompaniment to introducing the technology.

The truth, of course, is that none of us know exactly how this technology will be used in the future. We all tend to think about new technology in the context of things we have seen. With change as potentially sweeping as this, the new uses of the technology are likely to be discovered not by conscious effort but by tinkering. Some team, somewhere, will be facing a particular challenge or may be just playing around, and someone will say, "Why don't we try this." Lo and behold, this proposal will turn out not to be so silly after all and will work out pretty well. So well, in fact, that it will be worth trying out again in another circumstance. Eventually, totally new ways of using the technology will bubble up and be adopted by others. Someone will find a way of turning it into a product, and we will be well on our way to a new way of working.

Of course, it is always a little hard to tell your chief financial officer that you are installing technology without being completely sure you know how it will be used (and she should trust you, because you are confident that new uses will bubble up). The reality is that we will all have to justify the technology based on the benefits of using it the way we can currently imagine, and hope that serendipitous ways of using the technology make the payoff even greater.

Determining the Scope of the Program

All of us, when we are feeling just a bit inadequate anyway, like to kick the tires before we make a decision. When it comes to trying out new technology, the equivalent of kicking the tires is to "buy one and try it." While you *can* buy just one or two desktop videoconferencing setups, using those very occasionally will not give you a feeling of the efficiency that results from being able to turn to your computer and reach anybody in the organization—and maybe any major customer—with full picture and the ability to share text, access data, or hook other people into the call. "Anytime, anywhere" is what you are buying, and a couple of trial units does not give you a feeling for the benefits associated with that kind of universal access. In addition, you cannot really assess the usefulness of technology until you get comfortable with it.

A few years ago, Jim Creighton, one of the authors, set up an international professional association and attempted to hold board meetings by limited access chat room on a computer network that used early bulletin board software requiring that all commands had to be typed in. It was amazing the number of world-renowned Ph.D.'s who could not figure out how to get their modem to work. Then when they did, they would forget how they did it by the next time they needed to do it. A few years later, these same people are comfortable with the technology because they check their e-mail every day and access to the network requires that they just click an icon. At last it is really possible for this organization to hold effective electronic meetings. Getting effective use of the technology required changes both in the technology, to make it easier to use, and in the level of knowledge and comfort of the users.

The kicking-the-tires approach alone is not going to work because the scope of application is too small to constitute a legitimate test of the technology. But galactic approaches—approaches involving the whole organization and very sizable investments—have their risks too. A recent National Academy of Science report concluded that: "Bet-the-company information technology projects are likely to be overly complex, over budget, delayed and mismatched to customer needs by the time they are implemented."[1]

Although they all have strengths and weaknesses, here are the three basic strategies organizations are likely to use:

1. *Limited-impact modest change at the single-team level.* The smallest useful unit for collaborative technology is a whole team. Anything smaller than that misses the whole point of the technology. Some of the innovations we have discussed can be implemented successfully as a pilot project at a team level, so you can try things out and then make decisions about larger commitments.

Here are some observations about this strategy:

Advantages

○ It allows you to kick the tires before committing the organization to galactic change.
○ You can start with that team that is most enthusiastic and therefore most willing to put up with the inevitable challenges of installing new technology.
○ The team may discover ways to reduce implementation problems or to make the technology more effective that can be applied to the rest of the organization.

Disadvantages

○ Some of the technologies do not make much sense on a single-team basis, e.g., intranet.
○ The piecemeal approach is far more likely to mean that the technology will be used to support the way people

are already working rather than lead to new ways of working.

○ Providing total connectivity to even a single team may run counter to the existing information technology infrastructure—as long as you have to change it, maybe you should change it for everybody at the same time.

○ Judgments may be made about the benefits or costs of using particular technologies before they can be seen as part of an integrated approach.

2. *Galactic change, all at once.* Another approach is to decide that the potential offered by cybermeeting innovations is so central to your organization's success or survival that you will make the change all at once. This involves a major commitment of staff time and resources, and requires top-management commitment.

Some observations:

Advantages

○ It offers the greatest potential for whole new ways of working.

○ It offers the best opportunity to see how all the pieces work together as an integrated whole.

○ It provides the greatest potential for bringing about the cultural changes needed to support the innovations.

○ There is a potential for the greatest return on investment.

Disadvantages

○ It involves the largest investment of time and resources—if it fails, it fails big!

○ Early adopters run the risk of committing to technology before it becomes as user-friendly and well integrated as later generations of the technology (e.g., never buy software with a .0 in the name).

○ There are unpredictable consequences due to the amount of organizational change it kicks off.

○ The program may collapse of its own weight because it is too complex, too expensive, or too time consuming.
○ It may become a battleground for office politics.

3. *Some galactic, some single-team change.* This strategy commits to introducing some of the innovations across the whole organization, while testing others at a single-team level. Some of the technologies, like intranet, make little sense unless they are implemented organization-wide. On the other hand, other innovations can lead to significant improvements even if tried out in a single team. Most of the group process innovations can be used by a single team (as long as they are not significantly at odds with corporate culture). Desktop videoconferencing can certainly be tried out first in a team. Organizations can build one interactive meeting center before committing to building them organization-wide.

Some observations:

Advantages

○ This approach allows you to focus resources on those innovations that need to be organization-wide, while kicking the tire on others that can be tried out on a smaller scale.
○ The rationale for making the organization-wide changes may be easier to defend, with less risk of office politics.

Disadvantages

○ There is some risk that the program may not result in major changes in how people work together.
○ There is some risk that the program may not result in full integration of all the innovations.

Table 7 presents an analysis of which of the innovations discussed in this book could be carried out on a single-team basis and which require an organization-wide approach.

(Text continues on page 154)

Table 7. Analysis of implementation strategy.

Proposed Innovation	Organization-Wide Versus Single Team
Groupware that permits joint editing of a product— computer-supported collaboration	Can be used by single team, but not likely to lead to major process changes until introduced more universally.
Software agents that can carry out assigned tasks such as scheduling meetings or data searches	Can be installed for an individual, or for a single team.
Immediate access to databases	Internet access can be provided to an individual or single team. Intranet access requires a LAN (local area network). The value of intranet is based on organization-wide use.
Multimedia presentations/ modeling/simulation	Can be used by individuals or single teams.
Meeting room teleconferencing with participation of multiple parties at several sites	Can be used on a single-team basis. Far more likely to be used if it is universal throughout the organization and becomes an easy and normal way to conduct meetings.
Voice and written interface with computer	Can be used on individual machines and could certainly be tried out in a single meeting room first.

(Continues)

Table 7. (Continued)

Proposed Innovation	Organization-Wide Versus Single Team
Whiteboard working walls linked to laptop computers/ PC-linked projection screens	Can be used on a single meeting room basis. Far more likely to be used if they are universal throughout the organization and become an easy and normal way to conduct meetings.
Wall-size PC-linked projection screens/systems	Can be used on a single-team basis.
Use of thin-film deposit technology to permit whiteboard technology to be applied directly to meeting room walls	Not currently available.
Use of facilitators	Can be used on a single-team basis. Most likely to be used when it becomes standard practice throughout the organization.
Using meeting room walls as work space for group collaboration	Can be used on a single-team basis. Most likely to be used when it becomes standard practice throughout the organization.
Use of visual group memory	Recording on paper or whiteboard can be used on a single-team basis. Most likely to be used when it becomes standard practice throughout the organization.

Proposed Innovation	Organization-Wide Versus Single Team
Using graphic guides and process wizards	Currently graphics guides are primarily paper. Ultimately their effectiveness will rest on being able to select them using a software wizard, with the selected guide then projected onto the wall.
Use of process wizards and meetingware, keypad technology	Can be used by a single team.
Using team building to jump-start the process of turning a collection of people into a team	Can be used on a single-team basis. Most likely to be used when it becomes standard practice throughout the organization.
Use of interactive meeting rooms	Requires retrofitting of existing rooms or redesign of meeting rooms in new buildings.
Integrating project work space with interactive meeting rooms—the skunkworks concept	Requires a large investment in a facility retrofit or new facility. Can be done one facility at a time.
Designing informal social spaces to encourage informal and serendipitous interactions, e.g., hearths, team kitchens	Requires modest retrofit of existing buildings or inclusion in designs for new buildings. Can be tried out one building at a time.

Choosing the Best Organizational Strategy

So which of these approaches is best? The answers to that lie in the circumstances and organizational culture of individual organizations. In our minds, the crucial question management needs to address is, What is the value to your organization of improving collaboration?

Some organizations may be able to honestly answer that while it would be a benefit, the benefit is not so large as to justify an approach with downside risks. Other organizations may conclude that working effectively collaboratively is so central to their survival, competitive edge, or identity that anything less than full-fledged adoption of these innovations would be an unacceptable risk. Many organizations will lie in between.

While it's too early in the adoption of these technologies to conclude that there is a right strategy, there are some findings from a slightly different field that may suggest direction. Franklin Becker and his team at the Cornell University International Workplace Studies Program conducted a study of different implementation strategies for introducing "nonterritorial offices," or what has become more widely known as hotelling.[2] These programs were implemented at major companies such as IBM, Ernst & Young, DEC, Chiat/Day, and several Japanese and European firms. Becker's conclusions are:

○ *The planning process has far more influence over user satisfaction and work effectiveness than either the technology itself or the particular design that results.* The most important aspect of implementing innovative workplace practices is the process behind the implementation. In Becker's study, as the planning process became less intricate, user satisfaction and effectiveness ratings decreased.

○ *It is better to use the planning process at every site, not just an initial site.* In an effort to keep costs down, there is a natural tendency to want to go through a full consultation process at one site, then transfer the resulting solutions, cookie-cutter style, to other sites. But when this was done, just as many people said the change had made things worse or much worse as said things were better or much better.

A more satisfying approach is to work the kinks out of the planning process, not the actual solutions, at the first site, then transfer that process and a few basic principles, letting each site work out its own solution. The satisfaction rating was nearly 93% for projects where people adapted a planning process to their unique circumstances. The duration of the projects and the acceptance of the innovations was also much higher.

○ *The focus should be on how to work more effectively, not on how to reduce costs.* Those programs where the motivation was to explore new ways of working and to challenge conventional ideas of how, when, and where work should be done resulted in far higher user satisfaction (88%) than those that were driven primarily by cost savings (40%). Programs motivated by exploration/challenge also outperformed the cost-driven approach with respect to work effectiveness, project duration, and acceptance throughout the organization. Cost-driven programs tended to ignore the possibility of making fundamental changes in business practices, seeing the issue largely in terms of space allocation.

Those who wanted to find new ways of working were much more focused on the user. As a result, many of the cost savings from reducing space per person were reinvested in other functional work areas such as dedicated project rooms and informal meeting areas. This meant that the initial cost was somewhat higher than the cost-driven programs. But in the long run the cost-driven programs may have been more expensive, because they had to go back repeatedly to make changes in the facility and supporting technology.

○ *It doesn't seem to matter whether the innovations are driven by top management or are adopted by elements of the organization on their own initiative.* Somewhat surprisingly, this study found few differences in user satisfaction, cost, or acceptance between innovations initiated by top management to establish a standard for the whole organization, and those that individual organizational units decided to try out on their own.

○ *It's crucial to encourage consultation between the sites.* Although programs initiated independently by parts of the organization often proved as effective as top-down programs, little organizational learning occurred unless there was active encouragement of consultation between the sites. Without this, none of the lessons of hindsight were passed from one part of the organization to another.

○ *The presence of a strong champion is very important to the success of the project.* Most of the successful projects had a strong champion, and this was a particularly important element in determining the innovativeness of the project. The role of the champion was particularly important if that person was going to work in and share the space that was being redesigned. One of the major drawbacks of programs implemented by corporate headquarters was the perception that the people driving the program had little personal stake in the outcome because they were not going to be around to experience it. The idea that the champion is one of us and has to live with the consequences is a powerful message.

Top-Down Versus Bottom-Up

Implementing the kinds of changes described in this book is not easy. Every step comes in conflict with the habits and technology that already exist. This raises the question of whether it is possible to implement these innovations without top-down pressure.

Becker and his colleagues at Cornell found no significant difference—as far as acceptance, cost, and work effectiveness were concerned—between an approach that starts at the top and becomes the standard for the organization, and an approach that starts with the initiative of a single unit. However, the Cornell study might be used to justify the idea of a top-down *planning process* that made each organizational unit make choices about how, but not whether, it would use the new technologies.

Madison Square Garden is using a single-team approach

with an expectation of spreading the innovations to other parts of the organization later. A major reason for this is to start with a team that is enthusiastic and committed to making it work. But in our conversations with others, and in looking at the smattering of research that's available, we found a number of experienced people who believe that a top-down approach is necessary.

Bob Hoss, Worldwide Director of Telecommunications at IBM, has lived through the process twice.[3] Hoss, who has an information technology background, came from another major corporation prior to joining IBM. In the first company, the desire to use Lotus Notes came from a few user organizations, particularly the marketing organization. The information technology people were in a "go slow" mode because they knew their existing computer network was not designed to accommodate this kind of connectivity. Some user organizations could not wait for an infrastructure upgrade and moved ahead on their own. The result was that performance difficulties, outages, and support problems were commonplace.

Once it became apparent that Notes was becoming an accomplished fact, the information technology organization quickly provided the infrastructure to support it. Notes mail was eventually adopted as the standard by the information technology group but not uniformly or immediately by all user organizations. Hoss estimates that only about 20% of the company—primarily the marketing organization—consistently used the collaborative capability of Notes. The process of adoption was slowed by a lack of uniform agreement.

Hoss had a different experience at IBM. At IBM, CEO Louis Gerstner decreed that the entire company would convert to Notes. The role of senior managers was to ensure that implementation occurred in a way that did not break the company and that it resulted in as high a level of use as possible. Although there are still pockets of passive resistance—even at IBM there are still people who resist using a PC—the rollout is on schedule.

Although the decision to proceed was top-down, the heart of IBM's strategy is to make the use of collaborative technology so familiar and universal that people who feared it will find they love it and soon will not be able to get along without it. In particular, the strategy is to design the desktop so that when people log on they are already in Notes. Everything will be accessed from a single universal desktop.

Bruce Harreld, Senior Vice President, Strategy, at IBM, points out that every time people learn a new software package they have to learn a new metaphor, new navigation (how you move around in the software application), and a new language. IBM's goal is to design the system so they never again have to teach people how to navigate. IBM wants a seamless transition from application to application, from Internet to intranet, all using the same language and navigation. As Harreld puts it: "The last thing on earth you want to do is retrain people every time you change metaphors."[4]

Collaborative work will all be done in a **team room,** an electronic forum people go into to perform team tasks. All teams have to deal with certain basic tasks: setting objectives, defining tasks and schedule, assigning responsibilities, and monitoring performance. IBM hopes to establish a common vocabulary and basic processes to accomplish these tasks. Using this vocabulary and processes, teams may come up with very different solutions. All work done in the team room is available to everybody in the team—or anybody else the team designates for access—via people's e-mail.

Harreld has concluded, based on his own experience and the experiences of others he has talked to, that this level of change requires a top-down strategy. The CEO asks you to figure out *how* to do it without killing the business, not *whether* to do it. He believes you need either a directive leader who says "you are going to do it my way," or you need an organization in crisis. In IBM's case both conditions prevailed. When they converted to Notes the company was pulling out of a deep dive.

Harreld cites a story told by Darrell O'Conner, the author of *Managing at the Speed of Change,* about a major oil company operating an oil rig in the North Sea. As part of safety training the company had hammered home the point that in case of an emergency employees should never, never jump into the sea. The basic message was "If you go into the sea, you are dead." When a catastrophic fire occurred on the rig, only one of the workers on the rig survived. When an investigation was conducted, it turned out the surviving worker had been pulled from the sea. He was the only survivor because he was the only one who defied the training and jumped. His rationale was simple: Faced with the choice between a burning platform and the sea, he decided to take his chances on the sea.

Harreld believes that all major organizational change is driven by your customers and the marketplace telling you to change, a message that there is a sufficient crisis that you bypass the normal business model. One of the roles of management is to communicate this sense of crisis so that people will take the initiative to discover new approaches. As he puts it: "Good leadership is creating 'burning platforms.'"

In the authors' experience, major organizational change comes about *both* from top-down management and from innovations tried independently within the organization, then ultimately adopted by the whole organization. In the final analysis, the two have to link. Either top management champions an innovation that bubbled up from the bottom, or there is genuine and voluntary acceptance of the innovation pushed by management.

As discussed above, some of the innovations we have discussed could be initiated either way. But any innovation requiring fundamental changes to the information technology infrastructure of the organization, or requiring major changes in corporate culture, will have to enjoy the enthusiastic leadership of top management.

Principles for Developing an Implementation Plan

Here are general principles of implementation on which there is wide agreement:

○ *Consider the planning process as important to successful implementation as the innovations themselves.* As the Cornell University study reports, and as everything we have learned in the group process field over the past 40 years indicates, *process does matter.* User participation in decisions creates commitment to implementation. All the studies and experience show that participation in planning increases acceptance and use, and ultimately results in cost savings. However, in the short run, a process that includes potential users in planning will cost more money and take more time. Over time, this investment is paid back through successful implementation. Programs that are driven almost entirely by a cost-savings focus are likely to require frequent retrofits and efforts to force compliance.

○ *Focus the process on the user and the purpose, not the technology.* No matter what the problem is, you are far more likely to solve that problem if you stay focused on the problem or the user's need rather than the technology. There may be many solutions besides technology that you should consider first, or as part of a single reinforcing program. There may need to be changes in corporate culture and organizational reward systems. It may seem easier to fix the technology than fix the corporate culture. But so far, technology has not proven able to fix cultural problems such as preexisting animosities, unwillingness to share information, or heavy emphasis on hierarchy and control. If those are the problems, you had better address them head-on. Maybe in the process of doing that you will find that technology is a useful tool. But that is not the point of the exercise.

○ *Make all innovations as user-friendly, intuitive, and integrated as possible.* Except for a small band of people fascinated by group process or technology for its own sake, most people just want to improve doing what they are already doing. If they have to learn some new skills in group process or how to navigate in a new software, they may be willing to do so, but only if it promises to help them do what they want to do.

Once people have decided the technology might help them work better, the next question is, How big a barrier does the technology itself pose? How big an investment of time and effort is required before we get major returns?

Other preconditions for rapid technology adoption, in addition to a supportive cultural climate, are:

○ The machine must work in a way that makes sense to the user (it must be "intuitive").

○ The number of options the users face must be appropriate to the task they are trying to accomplish (they should not be presented with all kinds of bells and whistles they do not need to get their job done).

○ The way to move around and make choices must remain constant no matter where the users are in the software.

○ Users must quickly feel comfortable and at home with the technology.

It's no accident that the use of e-mail increased dramatically when (1) getting connected to the network became invisible to the user, (2) the machines told people they had mail, rather than their having to ask the machines, (3) decisions were reduced to clicking an icon or menu, and (4) people did it several times a day, so the procedure became habitual.

These principles remain even with group process technologies. People do not want to deal with having to choose 30 different ways of brainstorming. But here's where the technology can help: People are willing to answer a few questions about the task facing them and then let a software wizard present two or three options for their consideration. Of course they would be even more willing to do this if they could do it with voice commands or by just checking off a few choices on an electronic slate (at their seat, or on the wall).

○ *Connect all the key groups and players involved in the project or process.* It may make sense to start implementing collaborative technologies with a single team or process. But that team needs to have the tools to interact with all the other individuals or groups critical to the successful completion of its goals and tasks, regardless of whether they are in or outside their organizational unit, or outside the organization. This may include customers, suppliers, people in review roles, and organizational units in support roles.

The STRATIQUEST study described in Chapter Four found there was a consistent failure to identify all the people who were critical to the success of the project. When there were blockages, they were almost always with those individuals or organizations that were left out of the collaborative computing system. One team in particular was trying to design a very complicated product and tried to install collaborative technology at every department that played a role in bringing the product to market. Before they were through, they had identified 12 departments that needed to be linked for this team to be successful. Several of these departments were discovered the hard way, when the project got temporarily blocked because someone was left out.

This has important implications for implementation. Connecting a single team may require providing equipment, software, and training to a number of departments, which may be dispersed geographically. All of these sites will need continued training and technical support after the initial rollout.

The term that is increasingly used to describe all the additional people, outside the immediate team, who are essential to completion of a project or process is *stakeholders*. Stakeholders can include (1) people who must review and approve some aspect of a design or product, (2) people who control schedules, (3) people who control support resources (people, money, or technology), (4) people who can cut product or process costs or time if they will change their procedures or requirements, (5) people who are essential to implementation (e.g., marketing, customers), and (6) intended users.

Not all stakeholders need to be linked at the same level. The most important stakeholders need to be linked by technology or even by colocation (that is, a representative of the intended users, customers, or suppliers is physically located in team space, and included in all major decisions). Others may simply comment upon or review materials electronically. The team may need to connect with intended users by holding special meetings or briefings; issuing memos and newsletters; or conducting surveys, interviews, or focus groups. Obviously it is easier to establish and maintain this communication with intended users if some stakeholder-wide electronic communication mechanisms, such as intranet or Internet, are already up and running. If they are, all reviews can be handled electronically—software agents can take over the job of transmitting documents from place to place for review, and in the event of a need to resolve differences, agents can be used to quickly display comments and notify everybody of the need for resolution.

As veterans of implementing a number of organizational-change programs (not all of them technological) we would also like to pass on one bit of practical reality: *Somewhere during the process, something major will change—management, the environment, the technology.* The road to organizational change is rarely a direct route. Lay out your path as well as you can with careful planning. But keep your eye on the ultimate destination rather than focused solely on the step ahead—because there are likely to be some steps backwards as well.

Notes

1. National Research Council, *Information Technology in the Service Sector: A Twenty-First Century Lever*, pp. 19–20.
2. Franklin Becker, *Implementing Innovative Workplaces: Organizational Implications of Different Strategies*, Cornell University, International Workplace Studies Program, July 1994.
3. Personal interview with Bob Hoss, Worldwide Director of Telecommunications, IBM Corporation, September 9, 1996.
4. Ibid.

11

Collaboration Management

Collaboration and meetings—the most frequent form of col-laboration—are crucial to organizational success. As teams, rather than individuals, become the focus of management, making sure that the collaboration system of your organization is effective becomes a survival issue.

But who manages collaboration in an organization? In all the organizations we have talked with, no one we have met—although such people may exist—has a line on his or her performance goals saying: "Improve the effectiveness of collaboration in FutureTech by 5%." There are people in every organization who think about meeting rooms, or at least about office space that incidentally includes meeting rooms. Most information technology departments, at least in large organi-zations, are thinking about providing connectivity internally. There are people in many organizations who provide training on leading effective meetings, just as there are people who think about teamwork and collaboration. But nobody is in charge. There is no corporate strategy to improve collabora-tion organization-wide.

In some ways, *collaboration management* is analogous to *quality assurance.* It's the job of everyone in the organization, not just a particular department, and it's hard to get your hands on exactly where to start to make a difference. But in recent years, management has found a way to make dramatic improvements in quality, and it's reasonable to believe that similar results can be made in collaboration. It's a matter of focus. Management has to care, and ways to make improvements will then be found.

One of the challenges is that pieces of the puzzle are scattered throughout the organization. As a minimum, there is a role for information technology, for facilities management, and for human resources. Throughout this book we have referred to a number of important contributions that each of these organizations can make to meeting effectiveness:

Information Technology

○ Ensure that the connectivity infrastructure is in place to permit full use of groupware, videoconferencing (desktop and meeting room), Internet, and intranet throughout the organization.

○ Ensure that all corporate data is stored (data warehousing) in a manner that permits quick analysis—and can be reached easily through the intranet.

○ Provide training to staff in how to use the information technology infrastructure as a collaborative tool, not just for individual productivity.

○ Work with facilities management to develop interactive meeting centers that provide full technological support for meeting rooms.

○ Make constant improvements in the information technology infrastructure to make sure it is intuitive and obvious to use, permits people to access all tools from a single desktop, and uses a familiar metaphor and means of navigation—make the technology both as familiar and invisible as possible.

○ Recognize that technology won't solve interpersonal or corporate culture problems, so address these issues in planning any introduction of technology.

○ Form a partnership with human resources and facilities management to improve meeting effectiveness.

Facilities Management

○ Think "team" in all facilities design.

○ Create meeting rooms that can be instantly reconfigured for different purposes, under the control of the
meeting participants.
○ Create spaces for informal spontaneous meetings, supported by appropriate technology.
○ Create interactive meeting centers providing full technology and group process support where multiple
teams can reside for hours, days, or weeks.
○ Form a partnership with information technology and
human resources to improve meeting effectiveness.

Human Resources

○ Provide training in effective meeting participation,
meeting leadership, and meeting planning (see Figure
11).
○ Implement programs to identify and influence how
corporate reward systems and structure affect collaboration, and develop ways of aligning corporate culture
with collaboration.
○ Develop the skills and knowledge to be an effective
team member in designing programs to introduce new
technology. (This includes facilitation skills, knowledge of interactive group process techniques, process
design skills, and knowledge about collaboration and
human productivity.)
○ Form a partnership with information technology and
facilities management to improve meeting effectiveness.

These tasks may imply a broader mandate for each of
these departments than they currently enjoy. Under the pressure of daily crises these organizations get pushed into focusing narrowly on the challenges of keeping the system from
crashing, decorating the meeting rooms so the boss likes them,
and keeping the paperwork moving. Instead, each organization is being asked to broadly define its mandate in terms of
improving collaboration and productivity, and to specifically
make a contribution to meeting effectiveness.

(Text continues on page 169)

Figure 11. Training to improve meeting effectiveness.

Although high technology can play an important role in improving meeting effectiveness, do not forget good old low-tech training. Many organizations have received dramatic returns on investment—and more quickly than from information technology—by training managers in meeting-effectiveness skills. Here's some of the training you may want to consider:

Meeting Leadership Skills

The experience and training managers normally receive does not automatically equip them to be skilled meeting leaders. Some people, along the way, do acquire this skill, just as some people learn to become effective public speakers without formal training. But virtually all people can improve their skill with training, and many professionals and managers need significant improvement to do this part of their job in a fully professional manner.

In particular, managers need facilitation training. The role of a facilitator is to provide the structure necessary for the group to work effectively, without necessarily making decisions for the group. Facilitation contrasts sharply with more directive styles of meeting leadership where "the boss" runs the meeting, decides who gets to speak, makes judgments about everything that's said, and then announces a decision. Facilitation is particularly appropriate with project teams where a number of technical specialties need to be taken into consideration, or with cross-organization or multiorganization teams where it is particularly important to reach a consensus, since no one has the authority to impose a solution.

One of the key skills a facilitator must learn is active listening (also sometimes called reflective listening, or reframing). This skill consists of learning to summarize in your own words the thoughts and feelings of the person speaking, then checking out this summary with the other person. Although this skill is often badly exercised, leading to parody and well-justified revulsion, the lessons that are learned while mastering it are fundamental to business success. These lessons include recognizing that:

(Continues)

Figure 11. *(Continued)*

- The purpose of listening is to understand what the other person thinks and feels, rather than to concentrate on your own reactions or prepare your own response. (A lesson also fundamental for improving customer relations.)
- People may have radically different ways of viewing the same situation, which makes perfect sense given their own interests, roles, and subjective ways of perceiving objective realities situations. (A lesson also crucial to dispute resolution and to avoiding group-think.)
- People are more likely to change their feelings and positions when they feel their thoughts and feelings are being acknowledged and accepted (even if not agreed with) than they are when they feel resisted. (A lesson also fundamental to all human relationships.)

Although essential, active listening is not the only skill necessary to be an effective facilitator. Facilitators acquire numerous skills to restate problems in constructive ways, propose useful group process techniques or steps, keep the team focused on the purpose of the meeting, and resolve disputes.

Obviously there are different levels of training needed in facilitation. While every professional may find value from learning these skills, the need for the skills is higher among managers, team leaders, and frequent meeting leaders. A higher level of skill is needed by those who are recognized as meeting facilitators or those who are frequently in counseling situations.

Meeting Planning Training

The need for training in how to *plan* meetings is as universal as the need for training in how to lead them. Virtually every advantage of using the new technologies occurs only when people make conscious choices about how to structure meetings and which technologies to apply. Since most people have little or no training in planning meetings, they tend to revert to the "default setting"—meetings they have seen in the past and view as normal. It's unlikely that the full potential of the new technologies will be reached if people unconsciously select ways of holding meetings that predate and do not take into account the new technologies. Only when both meeting leaders and meeting participants exhibit a high level of awareness of the impact of meeting design upon productivity will improvements through use of the new technologies occur.

Meeting Participant Training

Typically we think of the manager as the person responsible for meeting effectiveness. But the reality is that in project teams, or any highly interactive group, some teams are more skilled than others at working together. Often the difference is not the leader's skills, but the participants'. There are definite skills involved in listening to each other, communicating concerns in ways that do not create antagonism, learning to identify core issues and interests, building creatively on each other's ideas, and reaching consensus.

These are all teachable skills. Often the best way to teach, though, is to teach whole teams rather than individuals. If a whole team goes through the training together they can reach agreements to use the skills, discuss and analyze how to apply the skills most effectively, and learn a common vocabulary that permits them to talk about their interactions. Training entire teams is a way of getting the team culture to support the new skills.

There is also a role here for the individual manager or team leader. Ultimately, meeting effectiveness will occur when individual managers:

○ Seek out training in meeting leadership and meeting planning.
○ Ensure that their teams are sufficiently familiar with the group process and collaborative technology so that personal discomfort or feelings of technological inadequacy are not barriers to their use.

○ Work with facilities management to create team space that maximizes the productivity of their group or team.

Collaboration Management

A key question is how to ensure that the behaviors described above occur when each contributor to collaboration has other responsibilities that compete for attention and priority. There are three options for achieving those desired behaviors: (1) the task force or team approach, (2) the issue manager approach, and (3) the new-function approach.

The Task Force or Team Approach

Many organizations start by designating an internal task force or team to address collaboration issues. The task force approach implies that there is a definable task and schedule. The task force might be told, for example, "Develop recommendations for how to improve our collaboration system, deliverable by [date]." The team approach also accommodates a continuing oversight role. That is, a group of key people would continue to monitor all programs to improve collaboration and report back to management.

The Issue Manager Approach

One of the constraints on a task force is that once recommendations are made and approved by management, the task force does not have a staff and budget to make it happen. A continuing team might be able to supervise staff and manage a budget, but team members will always face the challenge of competing responsibilities. An alternative is to put responsibility for implementation in the hands of one person who has a direct reporting link to management and whose job it is to oversee collaboration issues organization-wide, with staff and budget still residing largely in the existing organizations.

This kind of role is sometimes referred to as that of an issue manager. Organizations with issues management programs often identify an issue of such importance to the organization that they designate one person to manage this issue for the organization. Typically an issue manager is appointed when the issue does not yet justify a whole new organizational unit but is too important to leave scattered throughout the organization without some unifying control and direction. In many organizations, this may be an apt description of the level of commitment they will make to collaboration management: It's an important emerging challenge, it needs a unified approach, but it does not yet (and may never) require a distinct organizational unit.

The issue manager approach and the team approach are not incompatible. The issue manager may serve as the chair of the team. One of the first responsibilities of an issue manager is to create a cross-organizational sense of responsibility for the issue, and a cross-organizational team is an effective way of starting that process. The difference between the two approaches is that the issue manager spends full time focused on collaboration management and has direct responsibility for working with all parts of the organization to ensure implementation.

The New Function Approach

Some organizations may conclude that collaboration management is so central to their success that it justifies a distinct organization unit, somewhat analogous to quality assurance. This conclusion might be reached by a task force or team. The collaboration management department will have a staff and budget dedicated to program implementation. There is always a trade-off in creating a new organizational unit. The benefit is that the new organizational unit creates a sense of priority for the new function. On the other hand it may mean that other parts of the organization disown responsibility for that function: "Since there is now a collaboration management group, that's their job now, not mine." That's why the analogy to quality assurance is appropriate; the collaboration management unit has to instill a sense of commitment to collaboration throughout the organization.

The primary role of any collaboration management function—whether located in a team, an issue manager, or a department—is to ensure an integrated approach. Many of the pieces may already be in place, but not reinforcing each other.

Among the other purposes of a collaboration management function are to:

○ Create measurements, or "metrics," of collaboration, so the organization can assess how well it is doing.
○ Champion new collaboration programs both within management and to the organization as a whole.
○ Identify and maintain networks of people within the organization who are enthusiastic and willing to try out new ideas.
○ Spotlight successful innovations and pilot programs.
○ Provide linkages to collaboration research and innovations in other organizations.

The idea of a collaboration management organization is sufficiently new that it will be some time before it will be appropriate to recommend exactly how it should be structured and where it should be located in the organization. For now, each organization will need to experiment to find the right mix of "ad-hocracy" and structure to make significant changes in how people collaborate within their organization.

12

Fears About Collaborative Technology

Some people hate technology and swear that you will never find them holding meetings by computer.

To some extent this is a generational thing. Anybody who has ever tried to program a VCR knows that the only intelligent way to do it is to ask one of the kids. Our young grandchildren will soon be telling their parents how to find things on the Internet. Raised without fear of the technology, they just do it.

It's also a generational thing for many of the current class of executives who were raised during an era when anyone who typed was a clerical person. Executives did not sit at keyboards. Computers were tended to by white-coated scientists who lived in dust-free rooms. Many women executives avoided working at a computer for fear of being viewed as a clerical person. More than one senior vice president has been treated as a receptionist when she sat down for a minute at her assistant's computer keyboard.

Actually, the advent of e-mail has probably done much to break down this class consciousness. Now, rather than pride themselves on being "above" working on the computer, executives are embarrassed when they have to ask their secretary how to pick up their messages. Voice-activated computers will soon remove this embarrassment. But do not expect these executives to learn more commands than necessary to pick up their mail.

But the issue of comfort with the technologies is very real. A friend of ours helped design a meeting room of the future for a Japanese company. Each participant had a keyboard built into the table on which he could type comments that would be projected onto the wall. In addition, each participant had a laser pointer that permitted him to write on the walls without leaving his seat. Our friend reported, though, that whenever participants were excited about an idea they rushed over to the whiteboard walls, grabbed a flow pen, and started drawing.

One reason, of course, was that the technology was not a barrier. The excited participant did not have to think about the technology he was using (a flow pen). He could concentrate instead on the idea he wanted to communicate.

From our experience running interactive meeting rooms we have also discovered that when people are excited they do like to get up and move around. We can tell a team is really working well when we see people standing clustered around a board, gesturing, moving. "Sit down at the table" may make sense at the dinner table, but it constrains creativity in the workplace.

Using the new technologies will mean moving many people out of their comfort zone with the technology. Based on our admittedly unscientific personal observations, it took about ten years for people to become comfortable with voice mail. Now many people would rather leave a message on voice mail because they know it'll get through, without editing by a less than motivated clerical person. In order to succeed with a collaborative technology a person needs time to master it and become comfortable using it. The real payoff in productivity occurs when people do not have to think about the technology. They just know what to do to make it work for them.

This discomfort with the electronic technology is echoed in the discomfort many executives feel with group process technologies. Many people resist changing their listening skills, their meeting leadership behaviors, or their ways of approaching decision making because "all this group process stuff just isn't 'natural.'"

Of course what they really mean is that it would require breaking habits. Many of these habits go back to childhood, to socialization and training in school, to the years people have put in getting to where they are today. People talk about all the wonderful things they learned from participating in team sports. But then they turn around and say they cannot change that behavior because it's "natural" behavior. If it's learned behavior, it's simply a habit. It may be a habit that's been reinforced by a lot of success. It may be an extremely useful habit. But it's still just a habit. There is nothing inherently natural about it.

The reality is that learning improved communication skills, trying out a new group process, or acting as a facilitator requires going through the same period of discomfort as mastering new collaborative technology. A friend described the process of breaking a habit, such as learning a new tennis swing, as having four stages:

1. *Unconscious incompetence.* You are doing it wrong (your ball keeps hitting the net), but you do not know what it is you are doing wrong.
2. *Conscious incompetence.* You are doing it wrong, but at least you know what it is you are doing wrong.
3. *Conscious competence.* You can do it right—but only when you think about it.
4. *Unconscious competence.* You can do it right without having to think about it.

The real payoff from using either the group process or electronic technologies occurs when you have reached unconscious competence—you can use them effectively without having to think about it.

The survival value of habits is that you do not have to spend energy thinking about the behavior. If you had to think about every behavior you engage in to drive your car to work in the morning, you would probably never get there. You would be like the centipede who tried to learn a new dance step. Too much consciousness can be debilitating to productivity (just as too little consciousness can keep you repeating the same old habitual behaviors even when their usefulness is long gone).

The challenges facing a program designed to use the new technologies are to overcome the initial resistance to doing something "unnatural" and reduce the amount of lost productivity while people go through the "conscious incompetence" and "conscious competence" stages. If they do not get through it quickly, either the individuals or the organization will get so frustrated that they will stop trying.

Personality genuinely makes a difference in how willing people are to use new technologies. This is not true only of collaborative technology. Studies about the use of structured discussion procedures, for example, show that virtually everybody found they arrived at higher-quality decisions using such procedures, but not all the people felt comfortable using the procedures. People who inherently preferred procedural order found the use of formal discussion procedures more acceptable, independent of the outcome. People who liked less order preferred "free" discussion (e.g., discussion consistent with preexisting norms of behavior), even when the outcome was not as good.

Worthwhile Concerns About Collaborative Technology

Some of the resistance to new technology and new group process may be rooted in personal predisposition and resistance to having to break old habits. But there are a number of worthwhile concerns about the use of cybermeeting innovations that at least need to be acknowledged. We call them worthwhile not necessarily because we agree that they are valid, but because they have at least some basis in reality and are best handled by taking actions to address them rather than by denying their existence. Here are some of these worthwhile concerns:

○ *We'll become more vulnerable to technological failure.* As we were writing this book, America OnLine was off-line for a number of hours, and then was impossible to use because its new pricing policy totally swamped the system. A major node on the Internet was knocked out by hungry rats chewing on cable, blocking Internet access for Stanford University and a number of major Silicon Valley firms. These experiences made some people very happy that their computers were stand-alone and not dependent on the information super-highway.

Do organizations need to worry about vulnerability from technical failure? Of course. Connectivity does create increased vulnerability. These same organizations also need to worry that a competitor may be eating their lunch while they fret about vulnerability. Both concerns are valid. Organizations will need to design their information technology infrastructure with reasonable protection for technical failure. Most organizations will also need to get on with it.

○ *We will be vulnerable to hackers and industrial espionage.* That is possible. A whole new industry has grown up to address this issue. Again, the choice is not to avoid doing it, but to do it as wisely as possible.

○ *We'll spend all our time thinking about process and never get any work done.* This complaint is often heard about group process innovations. Since every group process has built-in assumptions about how people should work together, you can never avoid having process influence productivity. But having to rethink group process all the time does use up large amounts of time. That is the survival value of habits—you don't have to think about them, you just do them automatically. But if the habit is taking you down the road to failure, the only choice is to take charge of decisions about process that you ordinarily relegate to habit. It takes energy and conscious attention to break a habit. But once you have learned the new habit, it can be done without conscious awareness. The one advantage of having broken the habit is you never again believe there is only one way things can be done, and you are more likely to take responsibility for changing your group process whenever it is not serving you well.

○ *We'll lose our social skills, our sense of community, the personal touch.* If we try to perform all the functions of meetings using technology, we probably will. But the authors just do not think that will work. Certain basic functions of meetings, such as building trust, require face-to-face interaction. The focus on teams will actually increase the demand for the skills of working together effectively in teams. Once we all begin to use the technology, we will find new attitudes and behaviors associated with its use. For example, a whole new etiquette seems to be evolving for communication on the Internet.

People who want to remain isolated have always found ways to do so. But the new flatter organizational structures, and the use of temporary teams, will create tremendous pressure for more interaction, not less.

Organizations do need to think about designing new kinds of facilities that encourage team interaction when people are physically present, and about designing the information technology infrastructure so that a person in a distant location is just as present electronically as the person down the hall.

○ *Humans are being force-fitted into a mold to meet the machines' requirements.* Machines are not empty receptacles. They do structure the way we think and approach issues. The current operating systems for computers organizes information in hierarchical trees. When watching some people struggle with their computers, it becomes clear that this is not a natural way of thinking for some people.

Having everybody think the same way is not desirable. Our hope and belief is that the machines are becoming much more flexible, and will soon accommodate different modes of thinking. The pessimists among us will argue that the machines are not becoming more flexible, that we are just accommodating ourselves to the mold so it hurts less.

We do not have an easy answer. We suspect that anytime people create a new technology and change their beliefs about what is possible, it creates new possibilities in front of them, and drops out other possibilities behind them. We may mourn the passing of some of those possibilities. We may miss a fork in the path that would have led us to a fuller realization of human potential—or maybe just to a different realization.

○ *Having to work this way will pigeonhole our creativity.* This complaint is similar to the one above. Genius does not always fit the mold; genius breaks the mold. But for all the management jargon about paradigm shifts, real paradigm shifts do not happen very often and they do not happen on schedule, in budget. In the meantime the rest of us clods have to get some work done.

From our own experience we have seen the innovations described in this book lead to dramatic increases in team creativity. This is not just our observation; the research to date bears this out as well. Do these new approaches ask some people to work differently than they do now? No doubt. Is this a loss to them personally, or to the organizations for which they work? That's more in doubt. It's also possible that the new ways of working will reinvigorate, stimulate creativity, and result in higher productivity. That is the experience of people we have seen using these innovations. But maybe they were not geniuses.

○ *There's already too much information, and it's scattering.* A recent article in the *San Jose Mercury*, the "voice" of Silicon Valley, talked about mental health problems brought about by sheer information overload. Even those of us who are keeping our balance have complaints: Mailboxes are flooded. People compulsively check their e-mail "just in case" they have missed something. People seem unable to resist breaking off whatever they are doing to check out incoming messages. When your browser tells you there are 15,000 references for the key words you have typed in, it's hard to resist the urge to check out more of them than you needed to answer your question. When words can be changed at the flick of the wrist, it's easier to just whip them out without worrying too much about how they are organized.

We do not know whether the barrage of video games and multimedia everything has shattered the attention spans of our young people. They certainly ought to have marvelous hand-eye coordination after hours of destroying bad guys, blowing up buildings, or driving race cars. These young people may be better able to cope with their cyberfuture. But have they done it by accommodating to what the machines are good at, rather than by having the machines accommodate to what human beings are good at?

Of course the technologists' answer is that more technology will solve that problem. Software agents will prowl through the information and find what matters, will screen incoming messages, and will set up appointments without having to ask. Mostly we applaud the idea, but both authors are old enough to remember wandering through the university library and finding a book—a little distance away from the books we were looking for—that totally rearranged the way we thought about a topic. Will agents be designed for serendipity?

○ *We will focus less attention on the human dimensions of the problem, because our focus will mainly be on just what can be crammed into the technology.* This is one of the reasons we wrote this book. We are both excited about the possibilities of collaborative technology, and all the other innovations we see associated with it. But we are also worried that if the technology dominates, without equal consideration of corporate culture, group process, and facility, most of the benefits will be lost. In earlier chapters we reported on organizations that installed expensive collaborative technology only to find that it went unused due to interpersonal conflicts. Other organizations found the technology underutilized because it was at odds with the reward system in the organization. We also fear that the technology will reinforce old assumptions about how people work together that will make it harder for organizations to adapt to the changing external world. While we are changing the technology, let's simultaneously question the assumptions and build in more flexibility for human behavior.

13
Glimpses of the Future

To our knowledge, no single company currently uses all of the innovative approaches described in this book. However, there are several examples of how some of these elements have been implemented successfully—and unsuccessfully—by different organizations. This chapter provides an in-depth look at the introduction of these innovations at several companies, including one case in which old-time organizational culture got the better of modernization.

The first section concerns the intranet created by Silicon Graphics, Inc., which they call "Silicon Junction." This case is particularly interesting because Silicon Graphics uses the intranet not only for internal communications, but as a way to dramatically simplify and speed up administrative processes within the company.

The production control room for a television network is hardly the typical corporate meeting room, but at the Madison Square Garden (MSG) Network, the use of videoconferencing to tie together its production crews and executives shows the potential of this new technology to permit consultation anytime, anyplace. The MSG Network is the focus of the second section.

MG Taylor Corporation's DesignShop, the third section, is a three-day workshop that has been used by major corporations to make conceptual breakthroughs and co-create commitment to a new corporate strategy. DesignShop combines virtually all of the group process techniques described in Chapter 6 in a special physical environment designed to maximize collaboration (incorporating most of the principles discussed in Chapter 7.)

The final section examines the failed attempt to introduce collaborative technologies in a bureaucracy. The U.S. Department of Labor skunkworks intended to provide an optimal work space with supporting group process and logistics for cross-organizational teams drafting legislation and developing new policy. Unfortunately, the full vision was never realized, and the case instead provides a sober lesson about introducing collaborative technologies in organizations where collaboration is not the norm.

Silicon Junction

In 1993, engineers and programmers at Silicon Graphics, Inc., in Mountain View, California, began creating web pages for their departments and projects. This was not part of an official corporate strategy—it was simply creative people exploring the possibilities of the newly emerging World Wide Web. In 1996, Silicon Graphics employees were developing new tools for creating and manipulating 3-D graphics on the Web, and it was natural that they would begin to see the Web's potential for improving their own work environment. By 1997, their work evolved into what is probably the world's most advanced intranet, providing Silicon Graphics with a competitive edge in employee communications and productivity. It also generated a series of new tools which Silicon Graphics now sells as a product to its customers worldwide.

In many ways, Silicon Graphics is a natural environment for innovation. Founded in 1981, Silicon Graphics now has more than 10,500 employees and achieved annual sales in excess of $2.9 billion in fiscal year 1996. Initially, Silicon Graphics was recognized for its powerful graphics workstations. The company pioneered the development of visual computing by being the first to deliver a graphical user interface for Unix. Silicon Graphics also provides multiprocessing servers, high-performance supercomputers, and application software. In

July 1996, Silicon Graphics acquired Cray Research, and it now produces the largest range of computers—from desktop workstations to high-performance scalable supercomputers—in the industry. The company is best known to the general public for producing the hardware used to create the visual effects in movies including *Jurassic Park*, *Twister*, *Toy Story*, and *Independence Day*.

Every Silicon Graphics employee has a workstation on his or her desk or access to one nearby. Silicon Graphics workstations are powerful, and have the appropriate software to act as web servers. Graphics take a lot of bandwidth (the amount of information that can be fed through phone lines or network routes), and since Silicon Graphics focuses on graphics, bandwidth is not a significant constraint.

Silicon Graphics also prides itself on its openness and innovation. As such, the company does not monitor web usage. Silicon Graphics believes that employee trust will lead to rapid progression and development.

The growth of Silicon Junction required insight on the part of management. Silicon Graphics management observed an interesting thing: Employees who were most productive seemed to know more about what was going on in the company than others. When management explored why these employees were more knowledgeable, they found they were getting their information by exploring a burgeoning set of internal web sites.

Management agreed that the Web was a valuable tool, with the potential for global impact. In 1994, Silicon Graphics management created the Silicon Junction team. Its challenge was to support intranet exploration without trying to control it, focusing on sites useful to the majority of Silicon Graphics employees.

One thing was obvious: If individual departments across the company were creating internal web sites without a single, organized "gateway" to the information, employees would become frustrated at having to remember how to locate each site. The Silicon Junction team focused on creating the gateway from which all internal web sites could be reached. Employees weren't told what to put on their web pages. Instead, Silicon

Junction provided a uniform organization that helped foster the idea of one global intranet. The company also developed web authoring tools, a search engine, and other software that made the intranet easier to navigate. Some of these tools are now part of the Silicon Graphics product line.

The Silicon Junction team does not manage the content of Silicon Graphics's intranet—departments may post any information they want. Departmental "ads" that appear on the bottom of the Silicon Junction home page are accepted from employees on a first-come, first-served basis. If a department finds its site has heavy traffic, it can purchase a dedicated server for the group, or work with another department to move its site to an existing dedicated server. Additionally, groups with popular sites may choose to move their servers to an Information Services–supported environment.

The job of the Silicon Junction team is to make the intranet comfortable and easy to use for all Silicon Graphics employees, and facilitate web-based information access across the company.

The current look of the Silicon Junction entry point, Silicon Junction 2.0, is that of a polished daily newspaper. Users of a commercial Internet service such as America Online would be immediately comfortable navigating Silicon Junction. The home page layout includes a number of hot links that can be clicked on to reveal another layer of information or provide access to a variety of intranet services. When an employee wishes to locate different information, he or she can return to the home page and start again. An employee unable to locate something on the directory pages can launch the Silicon Graphics internal search engine, Sniff. It's attractive, effective, and simple to use. Additionally, the Silicon Junction home page includes daily updates of the most crucial and current company information and stock price.

Another major step in the evolution of the company's intranet was the recognition that it wasn't just a nice way to provide employee information, but a vehicle to simplify basic business tasks at a cost savings to the company. Silicon Graphics's intranet is now an essential part of its corporate strategy.

In 1996, many administrative processes and business

transactions were "webified." Here are some examples of how Silicon Graphics now uses its intranet to work more efficiently:

○ *New employees.* Everybody has had the experience of showing up for a new job, only to have it take several weeks to locate all of the basic supplies and equipment needed to work, and even longer to figure out who everybody is and where they fit in the organization. During this awkward period, employee productivity is quite low. This kind of problem could be exaggerated in a fast-growing company like Silicon Graphics, but Silicon Junction's employee services toolset has responded to this challenge.

At Silicon Graphics, when an employee is hired, the hiring manager or department administrator fills out a form on Silicon Junction showing who the person is, what his job will be, and for whom he'll work. The appropriate notifications automatically occur, ensuring that the needed equipment, supplies, and services are provided on or before the new employee's start date. For example, the facilities organization is notified of the need for a cubicle or office, and those who administer workstations know they have to set up a new system by a specified date. This doesn't require individual phone calls—it's done automatically once the web-based form is submitted.

○ Once on board, the new Silicon Graphics employee can fulfill most basic information needs using Silicon Junction. For example, if he doesn't know who reports to whom, Silicon Junction includes a web front-end "OrgView" that displays job titles, functions, and department and management chains up to the company CEO. Employees can also create personal web pages to post more in-depth information about themselves.

○ For employees who don't know where a building is located or in which building someone sits, Silicon Junction provides maps of the "campus" and mailstops. An interactive form allows employees to select their particular mix of benefits and submit it electronically to Human Resources. Administrative guides are on-line for many basic administrative functions. Requisition forms are available on-line to order office supplies. Employees can register on-line for training courses and select additional software from an on-line catalogues to be downloaded to their system. In fact, the information on Silicon Junction is so complete that employees can view the company's café menu while sitting at their desks.

○ *Meeting room appointments.* Silicon Graphics employees who want to reserve a conference room anywhere using a tool on Silicon Graphics's forty-plus building campus can do so on Silicon Junction. Floor plans are shown for each meeting room, along with its furniture type and layout, and its audiovisual equipment or collaborative technology features. Individuals can reserve meeting rooms while sitting at their desks by filling out a simple web-based form.

○ *Electronic requisition.* Silicon Graphics has grown rapidly over the past few years, adding several thousand new employees. As the company has grown, so have the demands on its Corporate Purchasing department—the number of purchase requisitions has skyrocketed. The traditional way to account for this increase would be to add more employees to the purchasing organization.

Instead, Silicon Graphics used the intranet to create a completely new solution. The Corporate Purchasing department created Electronic Requisition, a web-based front-end system that allows employees to search, request, and process office supply requisitions on-line. Employees choose from catalogued items using a "virtual" shopping cart. The completed form is then transmitted instantly to the approval hierarchy required to okay the purchase—those in the approval hierarchy can approve, amend, or reject requisition with the click of a mouse. The database even contains an approval proxy so if the person who would normally approve a requisition is on vacation, the approval form can be transmitted to a substitute.

Silicon Graphics estimates that the electronic handling of requisitions has produced an 18 percent reduction in cycle time for requisition processing, and a 25 percent reduction in average purchasing costs. The time it takes to purchase office supplies has been reduced by 82 percent.[1] The Corporate Purchasing department staff can concentrate on negotiating con-

tracts and selecting suppliers instead of mundane order-fulfillment tasks. Ben Gardner, Corporate Purchasing Services manager, estimates that his buyers can now handle four times as
many orders as before.[2]

○ *Advertising and applying for jobs.* Each company job
opening is displayed on Silicon Junction. Employees can view
and print out descriptions of job openings. Accompanying the
job information is a web-based form that allows employees to
update their resumes and submit them electronically to the
appropriate recruiter. This system ensures that everyone in
the company, regardless of physical location, is aware of job
openings. This not only encourages promotions from within,
but is also a good way to ensure that employees get the information they need to inform other qualified candidates, giving
Silicon Graphics a slight edge in the competitive Silicon Valley
employment market.

○ *Integrating databases.* In 1996, Silicon Graphics switched
to a new Oracle database that combined five separate databases into a single company-wide database. Since many employees were only familiar with the database used by their
organization, there was fear that the new system would require massive retraining. Instead, a group of engineers in the
company's Manufacturing Information Services organization
created and implemented a web-based front-end application.
The entry point into the database thus seemed natural and
familiar—employees were able to "mine" the database with
minimal training.

○ *Order fulfillment.* To meet its global needs, Silicon
Graphics created a web tool called Pole Vault, which allows
employees to make queries. Prior to this, a marketing person
in Germany who wanted to give his customer an update had
no immediate access to information about the status of the
order. With Silicon Graphics's new "Pole Vault" system, individual orders can be tracked by anyone in the company. By
using Pole Vault, employees can access part numbers, sales
orders, and engineering change orders. The individual employee in Germany can now tell the customer when the order
was shipped, by which carrier, and when it is scheduled to
arrive.

A limited number of Silicon Graphics's suppliers are given authorization to access the order-fulfillment system, so they can better fulfill the company's needs.

○ *Marketing research.* One of the major values of a database is its ability to store data and retrieve it later for analysis leading to insights about customers, products, or sales patterns. This is often called "data mining." Silicon Graphics has established a sophisticated data mining system—Mine Your Own Business, or MYOB Lite—which uses a web front end and accesses its Oracle database to provide useful marketing information. The tool is put in the hands of individual employees rather than centralized in the information technology group. Marketing people can create queries by choosing from menus that allow them to sort the information by nearly fifty variables. A marketing person who wants information about how a product has done in a particular region, and the demographic characteristics of the buyers, can click on a few items from the menus and create the appropriate query for an instant response to this question.

○ *Product introductions.* When Silicon Graphics introduced new products in the past, the company gathered its sales force at its Mountain View headquarters for training, at a cost of millions of dollars. Recently, Silicon Graphics turned to the intranet to fulfill these extensive training needs. Using Silicon Graphics workstations throughout the world, salespersons in remote locations accessed multiple layers of information, and were provided with whatever type of product information they needed. Using an internally-developed presentation tool with full audio capabilities called "WEBucator," employees taught themselves about products and potential applications at their own pace.

Evaluation of Silicon Junction

Silicon Junction looks wonderful on paper, but do employees really use it? Silicon Graphics funded an employee survey administered by an independent organization to determine how employees actually use Silicon Junction. The survey reported that 63 percent of employees use the intranet to obtain information required for their jobs, and more than 60 percent of employees consider the intranet essential to their daily job functions.[3] Users describe Silicon Junction as easy-to-use (85 percent), timely (85 percent), and accurate (92 percent).

Do the new intranet-based procedures save money? Silicon Graphics did a careful economic study of its electronic requisition program and found that it had a return on investment of 1,427 percent.[4]

Culture and Intranet Adoption

Lori-Leanne Parris, Silicon Graphics Intranet Program Manager, believes the 1996 acquisition of Cray Research provided useful insights into cultural differences between organizations and how they affect intranet development. While 80 percent of the workstations at Cray Research were web-enabled, only 35 percent were web-usable. This made it difficult for people to use the intranet as a work tool.[5]

Silicon Graphics has been working to promote intranet usage by Cray employees. The Silicon Graphics intranet was used to bridge the differences between Silicon Graphics and Cray's employee benefit packages. This involved registering benefits for more than 3,500 Cray employees. Obviously, this is accomplished more quickly when each Cray employee fills out an electronic benefit package form using the intranet than when it is done the traditional way. Silicon Graphics also sponsored a series of "Web Fairs" at Cray sites to get employees enthused about using Silicon Junction as a tool to improve their work.

Madison Square Garden Network Production Facilities

The Madison Square Garden Network is the oldest and largest regional sports television network in the nation, offering viewers live sports telecasts, up-to-the-minute sports news, and sports features. It televises both home and away games of the New York Yankees, New York Knicks, and New York Rangers—and on some days all three teams at the same time. The MSG Network recently constructed a production meeting room that, rather than resemble the average meeting room in Corporate America, gives some sense of how technology might be used in the meeting rooms of the future.

What you see on the television screen during an MSG Network telecast is the result of meticulous planning and an incredible amount of teamwork. A televised sports program includes pre-game, post-game, and game-time segments, and consists of live action, slow-motion playback, taped commercials, pretaped interviews and features, planned live interviews and commentary, spontaneous live interviews, planned cutaways, and unplanned interruptions for late-breaking news and events. It uses multiple cameras—most manned, some hand-held, and increasingly one or more remotely operated. Daily operations involve a vast array of talent in many disciplines, all working collaboratively to send the best sports television to millions of viewers.

Planning how all these pieces will fit together requires meetings, more meetings, and still more meetings. Typically—for each show—the program producers, directors, announcers, graphics and production people, and a host of technical people meet to lay out the basic approach. Then they work individually for a period of time, then meet again. Then they work in small teams, then meet again. After this meeting they rehearse, tape selected show segments, meet one last time, and then take their positions to send the show out to the cable affiliates. This cycle repeats itself for every production, and is always going on at MSG for at least one show— often, three or four such processes are going on simultaneously, preparing for different shows.

MSG Network had a problem. Its production facilities are located in a warren of cave-like concrete rooms tucked between the theater ceiling and arena floor at Madison Square Garden. However, as a result of network growth, the arena ran out of space to accommodate new people. So the executive and marketing elements of MSG Network were relocated to the sixteenth floor of an adjacent office building. This added

twenty minutes of round-trip travel time between the buildings for each meeting, with several meetings per day for each
person.

Joe Cohen, the Network President, and Mike McCarthy,
Executive Producer, realized that trying to maintain the established production routine would be a killer, particularly for
key management people. The new commute would run people
ragged and result in substandard performance. But they didn't
want to tinker with the basic production process, for as in
most television organizations, individuals at MSG Network
frequently work on the same team together in order to know
each other well and work together as experienced professionals. Once a company has developed an effective production
process, no one wants to disturb it.

MSG Network turned to technology to avoid this travel
time yet provide the oversight and decision making essential
to the production process. The solution was a state-of-the-art
videoconferencing link between control booths and conference rooms in the arena and the executives on the sixteenth
floor of the executive office building.

MSG was—and still is—going through an electronic infrastructure upgrade which includes desktop-to-desktop
videoconferencing capability for all MSG business units. But
since this upgrade wasn't scheduled for completion until the
end of the year, the MSG Network needed a more immediate
solution and more sophisticated equipment.

MSG installed standard coaxial cable to carry taped and
live programming from the arena control room to the sixteenth
floor conference room's rack-mounted video monitors. This
conference room is now linked through an ISDN based videoconferencing system to an arena control room and production
conference room. The room itself resembles a control center,
with racks of monitors and tape machines, a conference table
with conferencing microphones, a videoconferencing monitor
and camera at one end of the table, and tape storage cabinets.

Executives and managers located on the sixteenth floor
can now review taped and live television segments on demand
without having the material recorded on videotape and hand-
carried to their offices. The videoconferencing hookup permits

instant feedback from managers to production people in the arena and enables executives on the sixteenth floor to attend routine production meetings as they used to, but from the network conference room near their offices. Internal clients (people who place advertising spots or promote events on MSG Network) can also review and comment on work in progress without having to leave the area where their offices are located.

At MSG Network, the use of videoconferencing technology preserved the established and proven production process, kept the staff relocated to the adjacent building, eliminated the wasteful travel between the arena and the executive offices, and made life easier for internal clients. In this case, adoption of collaborative technology preserved significant elements of the company culture, but also served as an in-house demonstration of the new technology for the rest of the company. MSG Network hopes this will facilitate the company-wide adoption of the collaborative technology later this year.

MG Taylor's DesignShop™ Process

Throughout this book, we've emphasized the synergies that occur between the physical environment, group process, and technology. While there are many organizations that help companies design and conduct productive team or project work sessions, two organizations are noted for creating a combined physical environment/process design that supports creativity and conceptual breakthroughs.

One, the Eureka Mansion, is the creation of Doug Hall, a former marketing whiz at Procter & Gamble. Corporate giants bring marketing teams to the Eureka Mansion to create new product ideas in an environment that is designed to encourage creativity. Hall has described this process in his book *Jump Start Your Brain*.[6]

The other firm, MG Taylor Corporation, with corporate offices in Hilton Head, South Carolina, has designed a number of facilities known as "learning centers," "fusion centers," or "management centers." It provides clients with the option of bringing teams to one of its Management Centers in Hilton Head, Cambridge, Massachusetts, or Palo Alto, California, or having an entire MG Taylor team and physical environment brought to the client organization.

The "M" of MG Taylor is Matt Taylor, who began his career in 1956 as an apprentice architect and builder, working for Frank Lloyd Wright, Welton Beckett, Del Webb, and Tishman Construction. In 1974, Matt founded and directed the Renascence Project in Kansas City, Missouri, a futures-oriented research and community development organization that addressed urban renewal in the Kansas City area, while also serving as a school for entrepreneurs. He was one of the originators of the technique known as "fast tracking" and has applied cybernetics and systems theory to project work for thirty years.

Gail Taylor—the "G" in MG Taylor—has a background in education. In 1972, after teaching in Kansas City for several years, she founded the Learning Exchange as a center where educators could exchange ideas and rekindle their creativity and enthusiasm for teaching. Under her direction, the Learning Exchange became a successful, nationally recognized educational community resource center.

Over the years, the Taylors have developed and refined a process they call "DesignShop™" that is designed to help organizations make major breakthroughs. As they describe it:

> During an MG Taylor DesignShop event participants are facilitated through a rigorous process of exploration, co-design, assessment, and decision making. The power of parallel processing—looking at various issues from different vantage points and synthesizing the results of that examination—allows us to deal with the tremendous complexity involved in looking towards the future. A large group brings diversity, enabling the unique process to release the dynamic group genius.[7]

By using DesignShops:[8]

○ Carl's Jr. hamburger chain created a new design to be

used by its entire franchise for the next decade. Instead of going through what had been estimated as a $1 million two-year process, they completed the design in three days, and with sufficient internal commitment to cut implementation time by 50 percent.

○ Avis Rent-A-Car devised a way to use disbursed computer technology to expand the workload of its national reservation center without having to expand its physical facility.

○ An opera company facing bankruptcy found new ways to use its assets and was restored to profitability.

○ A government test center completely revamped its vision and business practices, replacing a 30 percent cut in government funding with $750 million in new business from the private sector, savings jobs and not only maintaining but expanding its expertise and capability.

○ Representatives of major American air carriers cut time delays by two-thirds in fewer than thirty days, allowing them to meet European curfews. This was directly responsible for keeping several major airlines from going bankrupt, and provided dramatic implications for revenues and cost savings. This DesignShop was sponsored by the Federal Aviation Administration.

MG Taylor's clients include such Fortune 500 companies as Ernst & Young, National Car Rental, NASA, General Motors, and the Walt Disney Corporation.

The Physical Environment

A team headed by Matt Taylor and designer Bill Blackburn has designed an entire line of movable furniture that allows you to quickly turn a large open space into an interactive meeting room. Much of this furniture has built-in whiteboards—although Taylor's boards, called Radiant Walls, are a soft gray that's less glaring and harsh than ordinary whiteboards. The main meeting space is formed by large, curved work walls with a write-on/wipe-off surface, which are on wheels so they can be quickly rolled into any formation. By wheeling around several of these curved walls, the Taylor team can create different types of work areas—from space for a small team to a general assembly area for groups of up to ninety. These work walls can be connected to other wheeled modules with shelves for television monitors, books, or other resource materials for the meeting. Smaller team spaces are created by connecting cubes with transparent Plexiglas backs that both provide storage and divide up space, or by connecting Articulating Workwalls™—Radiant Wall panels on wheels that can be mounted to most fixed walls, or to each other, to rapidly divide up space as needed. Tables, drafting boards, and even file cabinets are all on wheels so they can be quickly moved to wherever they are needed. Everything in the room can be instantly reconfigured to serve the purposes of the meeting.

The Taylors believe that fresh air, natural light, variable lighting, controlled temperature, a good sound system, artwork, and plants are all crucial to the meeting environment. In their own management centers, these elements are built into the facility, but when MG Taylor holds a DesignShop in a client's facility, a support team rolls into town several days before the sessions and transforms the facility into an optimal work team environment.

The Taylors design the space for variety and visual stimulation. Information boards or kiosks with the latest information on the subject of the DesignShop are placed throughout the work space, as well as toys, stuffed animals, puzzles, and balloons—anything to stimulate creativity. There are also materials such as Lego blocks and Tinkertoys that can be used to construct physical models.

The Taylors believe that this kind of physical space creates an environment in which people open up to new possibilities while remaining focused on the task at hand. As the Taylors put it, "DesignShops construct a complete environment for the benefit of your mind."

The DesignShop Process

The typical DesignShop process is three days in length. Although the Taylors originally limited their groups to about thirty people, in recent years they have found that the process is equally effective with groups of about sixty, and has even worked well with groups of up to ninety.

A DesignShop is structured not only to generate good ideas but to get a commitment to action. This means that the key actors—all the stakeholders who believe themselves to be affected by a decision—have to be represented. This can be a horizontal slice of an organization, or can just as easily be a vertical slice to ensure that all levels of the organization bring their knowledge—and interests—to the table.

Each DesignShop is custom-designed, although in general outlines they all follow the same pattern. Prior to the DesignShop sessions, the DesignShop facilitator—Matt or Gail Taylor, or other members of a network of "knowledge workers" the Taylors have trained—meets with the organizational sponsors and goes through a mini-DesignShop to define the problem on which the sessions will focus, and co-create the structure for the event.

One day, or several days, prior to the actual DesignShop (depending on whether it is at one of the Taylor's management centers or a client's facility), the MG Taylor team begins setting up the facility. This team consists of nearly fifteen knowledge workers, including the lead facilitators (often Matt or Gail Taylor), small team facilitators, and a staff whose sole job it is to create the unique DesignShop environment and provide the support needed for the event to be a success.

Because the DesignShop normally lasts three days, meals are served during the sessions (becoming part of the work time), normally while small teams are working on assignments. The first and last days of the event are scheduled to run late—at least until 8 P.M., and often until 10—while the middle day ends at 6 P.M. The intensity of working together for this prolonged period of time is part of the workshop design—it helps create a sense of shared experience and breaks down many of the barriers created by roles and normal business practice.

The typical design process is structured in three phases—*Scan, Focus,* and *Act*[9]—discussed in more detail here:

Scan

The purposes of the Scan phase are to:[10]

- ○ Immerse the participants in the critical technologies, facts, or concepts needed to get the team up to speed.
- ○ Build a real understanding of the environment—the markets, technology, and cultures—in which the organization operates.
- ○ Develop an understanding of the talents and knowledge of different team members.
- ○ Get team members fired up and focused on solving problems.
- ○ Challenge the assumptions on which current actions rest.
- ○ Develop a rich set of options from which the team can later make design decisions.

Ironically, during this phase participants are encouraged to avoid any explicit discussion of the issue or problem on which they are working. Instead, they are pushed to a higher level of abstraction and to consider familiar terrain from a variety of unfamiliar viewpoints. This way they are less likely to impose the usual constraints and standard ways of thinking on the problem.

The Scan phase typically takes the entire first day—almost fourteen hours—and sometimes longer. While the basic activities and group exercises have been designed prior to the session, there's no fixed timetable—the facilitators may shorten or extend activities based upon the interaction of the group. They also reserve the right to structure a new activity on the spot if they think it will move the group process in a useful direction.

Here's a progression of activities, drawn from an actual DesignShop sponsored by the Wharton School to identify the characteristics of successful organizations in the twenty-first century, that illustrates the typical activities that take place during the Scan phase:

○ The organization sponsor makes a brief presentation, outlining the purpose of the event.

○ The lead facilitator briefly introduces the facilitation team and the DesignShop process.

○ The facilitation team poses a set of questions, ranging from "What do you want to get out of the DesignShop?" to more provocative and complex questions related to the challenges the group is grappling with. Participants write their individual responses on large Radiant Wall panels.

○ Participants are divided into teams of about five, carefully selected to ensure a diversity of viewpoints. Sharing takes place by having each person locate the other members of his or her team. Each team member then explains the ideas expressed on his or her Radiant Wall panel to the other team members. While the participants discuss their panels with other group members, facilitators record their work. By the time the panels are erased for future exercises, everything has been recorded.

○ Each small group is asked to discuss questions such as "Where are our agreements and disagreements?" and "What have we learned about our individual beliefs and group beliefs?"

○ Each team is given an assignment that involves "backcasting," such as:

The year is 2095. The virtual history channel is planning a major retrospective on the last century. Your team has been asked to identify the major themes to be covered in the program. What was the character of the century? What were the major innovations or trends? How did these innovations or trends change people's lives?

Or a backcasting exercise targeted at a specific company or organization:

It's 2003, and your company has been out of business for the past two years. Describe the events that brought this to pass.

○ Participants reassemble in a large group and each individual is asked to report out on the most important trend, innovation, or idea from their group discussion.

○ Participants are broken into small work groups and assigned a "metaphor" for human organizations. Teams must think of their organization as an ant colony, river, rain forest, ship, beehive, ocean, human body, or garden. They are then asked to define the organizational requirements for success in their different metaphors, and what a twenty-first century organization based on these metaphors would look like in terms of strategy and structure. Each small team has an assigned facilitator and work space, and the facilitators assemble a mass of resource materials appropriate to the team's metaphor.

○ Each team presents a summary describing a twenty-first century organization based on its assigned metaphor, thus beginning the transition into the Focus stage.

On some occasions, the Scan phase is stimulated by a scenario or role-playing. For example, the new CEO of Agency Group—a firm that had sold insurance, mortgages, and other services in the same old way for decades—wanted people in his organization to think about changing the entire organizational culture. The opening DesignShop session consisted of a video in which the CEO announced that the company had just been sold to Mitsubishi, and that he was about to become the president of Mitsubishi America. Agency Group would have a new, presumably Japanese, CEO. Many participants believed the video was for real, and for the first time faced the prospect that their organization could undergo significant organizational change. This provided a powerful common experience on which participants were able to build for the remainder of the DesignShop.

Another company used a similar approach, announcing that the CEO had just joined another company and had taken all of the company's new product plans with him. This company had to not only come up with new plans, but protect itself from the stolen, competitive products that the people in the room had themselves previously designed.

Whatever particular assignments are designed for the Scan day, the purpose is to create a common experience and language, and get people thinking differently about the problem on which they will be working for the next two days. It is often an extremely frustrating day for task-oriented managers. As far as they can see, no "real" work is being accomplished—in fact, they're not even talking about the problem yet. Time is wasting. This meeting is costing a lot of money. At this stage, even project sponsors may be worrying about how to explain their decision to sponsor the event. On the other hand, most participants love the first day because they are intellectually and emotionally stimulated. Executives have little time to "play" with ideas and "tinker" with notions. Taking this time gives them a chance to focus on the real nature of the problem, and begins to change their thinking about the issue at hand. More importantly, they rediscover a critical element in the process of problem solving that they have been eliminating or drastically shortening due to stressful schedules.

Focus

The goals of the Focus phase are to:

1. "Invent" the problem.
2. Generate options.
3. Explore ways to decide which is the right one.

This stage consists of several iterations of develping a direction or solution, testing it by sharing it with other participants or analyzing it from very different perspectives, refining the answer, testing it again, refining, testing, and so on.

Group process experts frequently refer to the first step of decision making as "defining the problem." The Taylors prefer the term "inventing the problem" because they want people to restate the problem focus in a new way, taking into account the broader perspective achieved during the Scan phase. Once again, some of the task-oriented members of the group may have trouble resisting the urge to start trying to solve the problem, but the redefinition of the problem can be the most valuable part of the DesignShop.

For example, Avis Rent-A-Car started its DesignShop believing that its problem was how it was going to integrate a reservations center to be built in Virginia with its existing reservations center in Tulsa, Oklahoma. The Tulsa facility was rapidly approaching overload, and operating costs were rising. The apparent solution was to build a second center in a geographic location with lower costs. Property in Virginia was already being purchased, and building plans were being drawn up. Some Tulsa employees would be asked to move to the new site. Part of the challenge was to figure out how to split the workload between the two centers.

The backcasting assignment given to Avis during the Scan phase of the workshop was: "Picture this. You've got no central reservation center and things are running very well. The workload is way up, but costs are way down. How did you do it?"

As participants redefined the issue, the problem itself changed, and they then came up with a solution: By using telecomputing, the need for two geographically remote centers and for relocating people to another state vanished. The problem could be just as readily solved by working in mini-centers built in the low-cost suburbs of Tulsa. Nobody needed to move, and operating costs would come down. They had to think about the problem differently in order to solve it.

Inventing the problem typically follows a sequence like this:

○ Participants are divided into small groups to work on inventing the problem.

○ Each team presents its conclusions to the larger group, receiving a probing critique from the other participants and the facilitators. A central focus of this review is to determine if the groups have genuinely considered alternative definitions of the problem, or have settled too quickly on a particular definition.

○ Teams refine their definition of the problem, taking into account the questions raised during the critique, and begin to create a tentative solution.

○ Teams may then be asked to develop a 3-D model of

their proposed solution, using Tinkertoys, rubber bands, modeling clay, or anything else lying around the management center (much of which is there just for this exercise).

   ○ The teams reassemble and describe their models, once again receiving criticism from other participants.

   ○ Teams reappraise their tentative solution based on the critique received, refining it further.

   ○ Teams then reevaluate their proposed solutions from different perspectives in an activity called "authors." Prior to arriving at the DesignShop event, each participant must read a different book that the facilitators judge to be relevant to the discussion. There's tremendous variation in the books assigned, but all have something to do with complex systems, organizations, or new technologies. In the teams, each person is now asked to comment on the solution proposed by the team as if he were the author of the book he read.

   ○ Teams then refine their solutions once again, using insights gained from the different authors' perspectives.

Act

During the Act phase, teams develop detailed implementation plans and assignments for their proposed solutions. The Act step is put off until the last day in order to ensure that participants have really thought through basic assumptions, which can be very hard for people who can barely constrain themselves from starting to write plans on day one of the workshop. To these individuals, nobody is doing any work until the last day. The only problem is, you can't get to the unity of purpose and creativity that manifests itself on the last day without having gone through the first two days.

In fact, the lead facilitator sometimes opens the third day by saying, "Today will be 80 percent of the work." People are puzzled by this remark (since only roughly a third of the time is remaining), but so much gets accomplished in the final day because participants now have a shared language and purpose. That is not to say that the third day doesn't involve some struggle, but through the work of the previous two days, the problem has been clearly identified and the participants have built a shared knowledge base so they can move rapidly to solutions.

For the facilitator, the first day is heavily scripted. The facilitator knows the planned activities—although they are subject to revision—and has some idea of how long each activity will take. On the second day, a transition begins to occur. The MG Taylor team still provides the context in which the participants work, but breakthroughs in the participants's thinking often mean the facilitators do real-time redesigning of the session to better suit the participants's changing needs. By the third day, what happens in the teams drives the design and process.

In fact, the transition from the Focus to Act stage doesn't always follow a schedule. A key breakthrough may take place late the second day, or sometimes not until the morning of the third day—but at some point there will be a coalescing, a sense that the group has just agreed "we've got to do that." There's always a moment of insight, when the group realizes in what direction it needs to go.

The beginning of the Act stage is usually a full group check-in session, with each team giving a report of where it stands on its work. By this point, the team has developed an overall approach, and "kicked the tires" by testing it and retesting it using group critique, the model building exercise, and the author's exercise. Sometimes a breakthrough occurs during this reporting session, or, as a result of the reports, there's enough sense of common direction that the teams must be reconstituted for the final drive to develop a detailed plan.

This is also where the flexibility of movable partitions and furniture comes into play, as the support staff can quickly reconfigure the entire physical setting as needed to support the teams developing the plans. Working on the Radiant Walls is vital at this stage, as teams find they can create a common visual road map, working with enough space on the walls that the complexity of their solutions can be fully explored.

The MG Taylor knowledge worker team supports each participant team as needed. One team may need a recorder, another may want a visual model developed to organize their rapidly developing plan, a third may need research done on the Internet or in the MG Taylor library. Knowledge workers may also sense it is time to ask probing questions to test a strategy or proposed solution.

The last day usually ends with a large group session. It might be a report out from the teams, but it typically takes on the character of a celebration. Participants are often deeply moved by the experience of working together so intensely and going through an important shared experience. They need a final group activity to serve as a transition ritual back to the "real world."

Preparing the Journal

As participants leave, the MG Taylor team is gearing up for another round of work. If the DesignShop session has been held at the sponsor's site, there remains the major job of disassembling the environment, loading all the movable walls and furniture onto a truck, and taking apart the complex web of computers and other support equipment.

Another part of the DesignShop team has the job of creating a permanent record of what happened. All of the general sessions, and many of the team activities, have been videotaped. All of the materials written on wall panels or Radiant Walls have been recorded. Every diagram or model has been recorded in some manner. All of the plans have been keyed in and printed out.

All of this material is now assembled into a journal to document the DesignShop experience. This journal plays several roles. First, it serves as a touchstone that people can use to recreate their sense of common purpose. Second, it provides a timely record of the various plans to which people committed themselves. Third, it is a record of important ideas expressed during the workshop that weren't included in immediate plans, but which could be important later. For example, when Carl's Jr. was designing its new facilities, as a rule of thumb it only considered technologies that would be available within the next six months. Now, a couple of years later, other technologies that were discussed during the workshop are on the market and could improve the design or service even further. The DesignShop journal provides a trove of information that can be mined later. Because of its value, the MG Taylor staff works long hours after the DesignShop has ended to ensure that the journal will be delivered to the customer the week following the sessions.

The Impact of the DesignShop Process

The cost of an MG Taylor DesignShop varies considerably based on the services provided, its location, and the number of participants involved. A heavily-staffed DesignShop at the client's site includes upfront planning sessions, transporting the environment to the customer's site if necessary, providing a knowledge worker staff of approximately fifteen people, and preparing the journal. MG Taylor is committed to working with community organizations, and will co-design creatively to work with the budgets of community and non-profit groups.

Most customers express high levels of satisfaction at the end of their DesignShop sessions. The cost of bringing a large group together to work like this is modest if the sessions result in a breakthrough that defines a company's future direction, reduces by months the transition period from commitment to implementation, or generates a solution with long-term cost savings.

One indication of customer satisfaction is repeat customers. Several organizations have developed long-term relationships with MG Taylor and use the DesignShop process on a regular, continuing basis. Ernst & Young, the international consulting firm, uses DesignShops and exposes their clients to DesignShops as well. Lee Sage, the Ernst & Young partner responsible for its reengineering practice, believes that "In every instance, we're getting done in three days what we would have historically accomplished in somewhere between six weeks and three months."[11]

Ernst & Young is also using DesignShop principles to redesign its office space. In the past, offices had been 90 percent individual space, and 10 percent group space. Ernst &

Young now proposes to sharply increase the amount of team space to encourage greater interaction and collaborative effort.

Air Force Colonel Bill Rutley, who served as Director of the Arnold Engineering Development Center (AEDC), and later managed the program supporting the use of all F-15 fighter planes worldwide, has not only used DesignShops extensively at both locations, he's even had Matt Taylor design a leadership center at AEDC, creating a meeting space to be used for internal workshops. He's also had MG Taylor train the staff at AEDC so that it can run internal workshops. Rutley's predecessor at AEDC told him about MG Taylor when Rutley first arrived and, soon after, he met with the Taylors and decided to sponsor a DesignShop.

AEDC, which is located in Tullahoma, Tennessee, tests solid- and liquid-fuel rocket motors, conducts dynamics testing of subsonic, transonic, and supersonic aircraft, performs environmental space simulation, and offers other test services. It was built right after World War II, and still uses some equipment that was brought over from Germany after the war. Its customers are primarily from within the U.S. Department of Defense, particularly the Air Force.

With the end of the Cold War, AEDC seemed to be on a downward spiral. Military aircraft production had dropped remarkably. During the height of the Vietnam War, McDonnell-Douglas alone produced 72 F-4 fighter planes in one month. Production of all military fixed-wing aircraft was now down to 42 per year. AEDC was facing budget cuts in 1991 of 30 to 40 percent, and that looked to be just the beginning of the long slide into oblivion.

Rutley's first DesignShop was an attempt to produce a strategic plan for AEDC.[12] In the three-day session, Rutley and his staff hammered out a new vision in which AEDC would first develop new customers in the other branches of the armed services (although run by the Air Force, the original authorizing legislation made AEDC a service organization for the entire Department of Defense), while working to remove the legal and bureaucratic barriers which kept AEDC from getting more private industry clients. This strategy worked well, with AEDC getting legislative relief and eventually landing more than $750 million in new contracts, many from the private sector.

But Rutley had a major problem at the installation. A year earlier there had been a strike—there are a number of trade unions at AEDC, but the largest is the metal trades council—and although the strike had been settled, a residual bitterness and anger would occasionally manifest itself, and was always lying under the seemingly placid surface. AEDC's 3,500 employees were clearly divided into "us" and "them" camps. If Rutley was to get everyone pulling together in a new direction, he needed to do something to change this dynamic.

Rutley decided to set up a three-day DesignShop between management (much of it civilian) and labor. He himself would not attend because he knew that he couldn't resolve the issue with a command decision—it had to be resolved directly between the involved parties. He also knew there were some risks, for in the hothouse atmosphere of a DesignShop, there are considerable opportunities for confrontation. There was always a chance that it would make things not better but worse, though Rutley's personal prediction was that the session could only make things better. He believed that before things changed, everything had to be out in the open.

Since Rutley did not attend personally, he had to rely on his staff for occasional updates. At the end of the first day, his staff reported that they really didn't know what was going to happen. At the end of the second day, however, his staff was very excited, and reported that they thought there had been a breakthrough. They asked him to be at the session the next morning, but refused to tell him why.

When he arrived the next morning, he learned that there had in fact been a major confrontation which had in turn led to an acknowledgment of responsibility on both sides, and a commitment to "bury the hatchet."

DesignShop staff decided to take the phrase "bury the hatchet" quite literally. One knowledge worker had convinced her husband to make a gorgeous little casket, just large enough to hold an actual hatchet. The casket lid had enough holes drilled in it for each DesignShop participant to drive a nail through. Another part of the team drafted a covenant committing to starting anew.

The next day, the participants noticed something unusual when funeral music began to play. Soon a staffer dressed as the Grim Reaper led a procession into the room, followed by pallbearers carrying the casket, all dressed in black and wailing. The Grim Reaper asked everyone in the room to sign the covenant to bury the hatchet, and the original was placed in the coffin. Then everyone hammered a nail into the coffin lid. Both labor and management representatives were assigned as pallbearers to carry the casket to a black car waiting outside, with an official AEDC police car in front of it.

The funeral procession wound through the base and, as is the custom in the South, other cars stopped and the passengers got out to pay their respects to the deceased. Soon the procession arrived at a spot near the front entrance of AEDC that had been marked for the burial. Everyone took shovels and dug a hole for the casket. There was a brief ceremony, with everyone singing "Nearer My God to Thee." Later on, a permanent headstone was installed at the burial site, and can still be seen today, about 100 yards inside the main entrance to AEDC.

Rutley reports that the Center changed fundamentally that day. While the funeral probably seemed hokey to some, because it flowed out of the intense experience of the DesignShop it was no surprise to find some of the participants in tears during the ceremony. For them, burying the hatchet had become real. It still took work to completely transform the "us" versus "them" mentality among 3,500 employees, but the change began that day and has been largely successful.

Rutley also used DesignShops to initiate the increase of the amount of work in the F-15 program managed by private companies. The military management of the F-15 program, and the three large corporate contractors that support it, participated in a DesignShop in which they hammered out an agreement called "Intelligent Partnering." Its basic premise is that either extreme—total government operation or total private operation—is unintelligent. The challenge was to agree on "Who ought to do it?" (which Rutley refers to as the "efficiency" criteria) and "How should it be done?" (the "effectiveness" criteria). This was worked out in the context of three earthy rules:

1. Whatever you do, don't screw up the war fighter (pilot).
2. Don't screw the taxpayer.
3. Don't screw people (government or contractor).

In actuality, many of the changes resulting from this DesignShop will be "in place"—that is, with the same employees performing the work but different management. The thrust of the program is to have government employees doing the work they do best and protecting taxpayers, while private industry performs the work it does best.

Rutley found it easier to use DesignShops at AEDC because all the staff was on-site. The F-15 program is scattered around the world, and supports fighter aircraft somewhere in the world twenty-four hours a day, seven days a week, so he can only bring key staff together once every six months. This constraint has less to do with the costs of the DesignShop than with the program costs of gathering key staff for a minimum of one week (with travel time) from all around the world. If Bill Rutley had his druthers, he would hold DesignShops much more often—AEDC is a testament to their effectiveness.

Future Directions

While MG Taylor has had their Management Centers for twenty years, they are now adding new centers and offering a broader range of services and products—in particular, new retail space called KnOwhere Stores, in which you can develop a business plan, purchase books, art tools, and toys, or outfit a work environment with the full line of MG Taylor Work Furniture™ and WorkWalls™. There are KnOwhere Stores in Hilton Head Island, South Carolina, and Cambridge, Massachusetts. The Palo Alto, California KnOwhere Store opened in August 1997, and features an "incubator" space—a space where a team can assemble to create a new product or hatch a new organization. Work spaces will provide both privacy and interaction with others in the space. There will also be hoteling space in which an individual—such as an author working on a book—can have a work area for an independent project.

U.S. Department of Labor Skunkworks

This section might be subtitled "How the Skunkworks Got Skunked," because it concerns an innovative meeting facility that never lived up to its potential. The space still exists, but its current use is a mere shadow of the original vision. To our mixed pride and embarrassment, this is a project in which co-author Jim Creighton's firm, Creighton & Creighton, Inc., was involved. It was the Cinderella story backwards: What looked like a vision of loveliness turned into something far less.

Beginnings

The story of the Department of Labor skunkworks begins during the transition period when President Bush was finishing his term and the Clinton Administration was putting together the team that would take over the reins of government. At the time, the transition team was housed in a large, open building, which was formerly a warehouse. All of the incoming Secretaries and their staff were housed in the same facility. Future Secretary of Labor Robert Reich would sit on a table, and he and his assigned transition team would have intense discussions about the future direction of the Department of Labor. If people who were working on issues related to other departments happened by and wanted to join the discussion, so much the better. This openness led to cross-fertilization and the insights that occur when people approach an issue from very different perspectives. Bob Reich loved all the give and take—it was like a college bull session, only with very intelligent, experienced people, who cared passionately about the issues.

Everything changed when Reich officially became Secretary of Labor. He now occupied a huge office (with a truly sensational view of the U.S. Capitol). Getting in to see him meant going through security downstairs, then getting past a phalanx of secretaries and assistants in the outer office. Policy development was no longer an exciting intellectual discussion—proposals worked their way up and down well-defined and well-defended organizational stovepipes. Although there were frequent turf wars, there was little give and take and stimulating byplay. Reich missed the excitement of the transition.

Reich, the author of a number of books on labor and management issues, and a student of management theory, was convinced that a team approach was superior, and was familiar with the story of the famed Lockheed Aircraft skunkworks. After World War II, Lockheed Aircraft grew quickly and soon found that, with growth and age, there was a clogging of the arteries when it came to designing exciting new airplanes. Things weren't getting done because of too much bureaucracy. So Lockheed management took creative people from each department and formed them into an advanced design team. This team could make commitments for the organizations its members represented. Their designs counted. And soon, they began to design many of the most famous post-war military planes. Because they were located across the street from a particularly stinky chemical factory, the building began to be called the "skunkworks," after the "skonkworks," an illegal whiskey still maintained by one of the characters in Al Capp's well-known L'il Abner cartoon. The name stuck, and people soon forgot the official name of the facility.

Reich's vision was somewhat similar—instead of having policy slowly work its way through the various parts of the Department, he would create a facility where teams of people drawn from all the crucial organizational units would work together on a crash basis to formulate policy or draft legislation. This space would be big enough for several teams to occupy it at the same time. Some teams might stay a few weeks, others might be there for months. The space would be designed for interaction and to support creativity.

Since the teams would primarily be working on policy issues, Reich assigned the project to the Assistant Secretary for Policy, who in turn assigned the project to Roland Droitsch, a Deputy Assistant Secretary (DAS). In the Department of Labor, each assistant secretary typically has two deputy assistant secretaries who report to him or her—one a political appointee, the other a career civil service employee. Droitsch was the civil service Deputy Assistant Secretary.

The skunkworks was to be carved out of existing office space across the hall from Secretary Reich's office. It first involved clearing out the existing occupants of the space, which caused some hard feelings since space so close to the Secretary's office is highly prized. Droitsch and his immediate staff then set about creating the space and ordering movable open-office furniture and partitions, new computers, and the latest groupware, Lotus Notes, which had just come on the market.

These were actually heady times for the Department of Labor. President Clinton had been elected in part because voters had decided that Bush was out of touch with domestic problems. The public was disturbed by a drumbeat of news stories about layoffs. There were so many layoffs that corporations relabeled them as "downsizing" to make them more palatable, but the public knew they were still layoffs, and was deeply concerned.

The Clinton Administration diagnosed the problem as a fundamental shift in the economic structure, part of the transition from the Industrial Age to the Information Age. There really was a difference between "layoffs" and "downsizing." With layoffs, there was some hope that jobs would be restored when the economy got better. With downsizing, the jobs were gone forever. Industrial workers making $20 an hour would be lucky to find new jobs at $10 an hour. College-educated middle managers now found themselves pounding the sidewalks looking for work.

The solution, the Clinton Administration felt, was not just reeducation but continuous education. Also, the unemployment benefits system needed to be rethought—the system was designed to bridge people from one job to the next, not to cope with people whose jobs had disappeared completely. All of these issues were Labor Department issues, so Secretary Reich and his team came in with expectations that the Labor Department would be playing a challenging and exciting role in creating major new initiatives. In fact, the first team to enter the skunkworks was a team Reich set up to draft proposed legislation on how to address the problems of "dislocated workers," people whose jobs had simply disappeared.

The problem was that the physical setting of the skunkworks was not quite ready, and there was no mechanism in place to provide the support necessary to run the center. Roland Droitsch had submitted a $300,000 budget request for support services, but was stunned when he got only $10,000. A veteran of many years in the bureaucracy, Droitsch scraped together $100,000 from a variety of sources. He hoped that this money would give the skunkworks time to prove its worth, at which point more funding would be available.

But the period of uncertainty while Droitsch was searching for the money used up the time needed to go through the competitive bidding process to select a contractor. By the time the money was together, the first team was ready to enter the skunkworks, and others were lining up right behind.

The Next Step

Jim Jones had an idea. Jones was a senior staff member of the Office of Policy, who occupied one of a row of permanent offices which opened onto the skunkworks and were occupied by internal consultants who served as the Department's subject matter experts on key labor issues. He was in charge of setting up the Department's Alternative Dispute Resolution (ADR) program (ADR is an effort to find ways of resolving disputes by means other than litigation). Jones had headed a pilot program in Labor's Philadelphia Office to assess whether the use of mediation would be an effective approach to resolving claims and other disputes. The program had shown such dramatic results that Jones had asked to plan a similar program for the entire Department of Labor. Through Jones's contacts with other agencies using ADR, Droitsch learned that the U.S. Army Corps of Engineers had a contract with Creighton & Creighton, a firm experienced not only in dispute resolution, but in facilitation, partnering, meeting design, stakeholder participation, and managing crash projects.

Droitsch proposed that Labor transfer money to the Corps of Engineers, and have the Corps arrange for this contractor to provide support services for the skunkworks on a temporary basis. The Corps was willing, particularly since it had some ongoing disputes with other parts of the Labor Department on wage/hour issues, and hoped to use the skunkworks for joint Corps-Labor partnering activities. The Corps would provide its consultant, who would not only manage the skunkworks under Labor's direction but begin setting up a process for resolving issues between the Corps and Labor.

The Corps of Engineers has for years been a leader in the use of Alternative Dispute Resolution. In the late 1980s, Lester Edelman, the General Counsel of the Corps, awakened to the fact that he headed one of the largest legal staffs in the world, second only to the Internal Revenue Service. He realized that the growing use of litigation to resolve almost every dispute had to be curbed. This could only be done by turning responsibility for dispute resolution back to line managers, providing them with new tools for effective resolution. Edelman turned to the Corps's policy think tank, the Institute for Water Resources, to set up and implement an agency-wide ADR program. With considerable expertise but limited staff, the Institute went through a competitive bidding process to obtain the services of a firm to develop training, prepare manuals and guides, conduct research and case studies, and provide direct technical assistance. The Corps selected a team of consultants headed by Creighton & Creighton, Inc., which had provided services to the program continuously since 1989 (having won successive contracts).

Our Contribution

Creighton & Creighton was thrilled with the skunkworks project. It was a chance to put into practice almost everything they had learned in nearly thirty years of consulting. Just before Christmas in 1993, Jim Creighton met with Roland Droitsch to plan how to provide support for the skunkworks. Creighton also met with the leader of the first team, which was already occupying the space. She was extremely upset. She felt Secretary Reich had promised her an optimal meeting space, and instead she had a meeting space with absolutely no support. Even making photocopies was a major exercise. Creighton told her that the paperwork was in the mill, and that he hoped to put staff in place right after the Christmas holidays. Creighton also talked with several leaders of other prospective teams.

Snags

Things did not go as planned. Instead, miscommunication between Labor and the Corps resulted in a two-month delay in getting the paperwork approved. By the time Creighton got the go-ahead to put staff in place, the first team was very upset and angry. To speed up the process, Creighton took on the job of hammering out the overall strategic plan for the Center, while his partner (and wife) Maggie Creighton took on the task of hiring and training support staff to provide logistics and clerical support.

Also in the interim, Mark Hunker, a new political appointee, had been placed in charge of the skunkworks. The previous Assistant Secretary had been moved to another position in the Secretary's Office, and the politically-appointed Deputy Assistant Secretary was the Acting Assistant Secretary, with Hunker reporting to her. Droitsch was still involved and interested in the skunkworks, but the real chain of command was developing through the political side of the house reporting directly to the Acting Assistant Secretary.

Solutions

Jim Creighton convened a two-day design session bringing together key Labor Department staff (including Hunker and

Jones) and a "braintrust" of outside consultants. Creighton & Creighton manages large projects by putting together teams of consultants with specialized skills and prior experience working together. For this project, Creighton pulled together a team which included: Jim Channon, former head of futures studies for the U.S. Army and a brilliant visual recorder; Paul Grabhorn, who'd been part of a team that designed a "meeting room of the future" for a Japanese group and was also an expert at producing outstanding computer-generated reports and graphics; Langdon Morris, an architect who had worked previously with Matt Taylor on the design of the Taylors's meeting room furniture and was himself an author on changing organizational structures;[13] and Bill Robertson, then Deputy Chief of the Corps of Engineers and head of its Office of Strategic Initiatives, and now acting CEO of a major international consulting firm.

The vision of the skunkworks which had been developing, and which this team supported, included these elements:

○ The skunkworks could provide work space for about eighteen people, whether members of a single team or several smaller teams. Each workstation would include the then-latest computer (Pentium 486) with Lotus Notes.

○ The skunkworks floor plan included a large alcove which created a natural meeting space, appropriate for whiteboard walls on three sides. Other meeting spaces would need to be carved out of a large open space by using movable dividers. Smaller project team space could be created with the open-space furniture already on hand. Langdon Morris would develop several options for its ultimate design (see Figure 9).

○ The skunkworks coordinator would meet with the leader of each proposed new team several weeks prior to its entry into the facility. They would then identify the services to be provided, including the level of logistics support needed. Some teams would bring additional clerical staff with them, others would not.

○ Each entering team would go through a team building/strategic planning session, facilitated by Creighton &

Creighton facilitators. Additional process design and facilitation services would be provided to the team upon request. Creighton & Creighton would also provide dispute resolution services if needed.

○ Some teams would need to consult with other stakeholders throughout the agency and in other agencies. Creighton & Creighton could support them in designing their stakeholder involvement programs, and assist with putting on major events such as large workshops or meetings, which could also be done in the skunkworks.

○ Creighton & Creighton would provide two full-time clerical people in the center, as well as an overall coordinator who would be the contact for scheduling services and arranging for customer support.

○ The skunkworks could also be reconfigured for major meetings or ceremonial events scheduled by Secretary Reich.

○ The Department's internal consultants, housed in offices which opened on the skunkworks, could be assigned as full members of teams, or could be drawn in as subject matter experts when teams needed them.

All of this was new for Mark Hunker, a public accountant who had been appointed to his present position based on his service during President Clinton's campaign. He'd been in the White House as part of a team that made key appointments for the Administration, and after that had arranged his appointment to Labor. He was a good administrator, but had no prior experience with facilitation, group process, or facility design. He was trying to be supportive, but it was clear that the political appointees were very anxious about the skunkworks, and he was repeatedly being questioned on minute expenditures.

More Hard Work

Meanwhile, Maggie Creighton was hard at work getting the support staff trained and in place. Since she didn't know people in the Department, arranging for any service required research just to find out who was in charge. She was advised by other Department of Labor staff that, to put it politely, "Labor does not have a customer service orientation." Perhaps it was just as well she was not part of the culture, because by going directly to people and laying out her problem she was getting things done in hours that were expected to take months. For example, when noise problems made the alcove meeting space too noisy for effective work, she located the person in charge of office furniture and found that instead of going through weeks of formal approvals she could have movable dividers the same afternoon, as long as she didn't care which shade of red she got.

For the next few months, Maggie Creighton and her team lived and breathed skunkworks, often putting in fourteen-hour days. The teams using the skunkworks were working just as hard—operations were on an almost twenty-four-hour-a-day footing. Maggie and her team were finally regaining the confidence of the resident teams, who, for the first time, were seeing the skunkworks as a great place to work. Other teams began to use the skunkworks, some just for meetings, others for short-term residence. Over time, teams working on such issues as workplace ergonomics, steel erection standards, tuberculosis, child labor, and drugs in the workplace used the facility. The White House called and wanted to use the skunkworks to organize a major ceremony to celebrate the signing of a bill involving the Labor Department. Maggie and her team poured on the hours, and immediately after the event were thanked and toasted by Secretary Reich, who supplied the champagne.

Teams also began to appreciate the value that a facilitator/process consultant could bring to their efforts. Maggie facilitated several strategic planning or team building sessions, including some where significant disputes had broken out in one of the teams. Teams particularly liked the wall-sized strategic planning process charts (refer back to Figure 6 on page 84), which provided a structure they could go through almost by themselves, and which they found helpful as a visual reminder of where they were in the process.

Eventually, Maggie was able to return to her California

home with a highly competent coordinator and skilled logistical staff in place, serving their skunkworks customers with a well-developed customer service attitude.

What she didn't know was that the skunkworks had already experienced its moment of glory. The Department was in a cost-cutting mood, and Mark Hunker was ordered to cut costs. He liked Langdon Morris's floor plan, but wasn't going to pay the kind of money that Morris's movable curved working walls would cost, nor was he willing to pay the cost of changing the electrical infrastructure of the room. Also, there were fewer and fewer calls to the Creightons asking them to provide professional facilitators. The Creightons's on-site coordinator facilitated a few team meetings, and Hunker even took a stab at it. Eventually, things settled into a pattern where Creighton & Creighton provided the coordinator and logistics staff, but did little else. Jim Creighton tried once to talk to Hunker about the value of facilitation and group process, but Hunker wasn't about to pay for anything.

The team that was drafting legislation to help "downsized" workers was still there, although its purpose had changed. It had successfully drafted legislation, under very rigid time pressures, and was now working on selling the legislation. With this change in purpose came a new team leader. The original team leader had effectively held the team together, and it produced a prodigious amount of work. However, the new team leader was so arrogant and brash that he alienated all the other team members and the skunkworks support staff in less than twenty-four hours.

The Finale

By now the political climate had changed as well. Faced with a need to bring the budget deficit under control, the White House was cutting programs, not adding them. In November, the Republicans had taken control of Congress, and the new Congress was not about to fund expensive new education programs. The economy was doing well, and the public was less concerned about downsizing companies. The action had shifted away from the Labor Department.

Secretary Reich, faced with a split developing in the team, and looking at the external political climate, decided not to intervene to improve the workings of the team—he simply shut the team down. He also seemed to lose interest in the skunkworks itself, sponsoring no additional teams. Teams were still welcome to come into the skunkworks, but they had to bring their checkbooks with them to pay for the services they used. Several teams considered it, but ultimately backed off as budget cuts in the Department got worse and worse.

By the end of the year, the task order under which Creighton & Creighton was operating came to an end. The Creightons made sure that their coordinator landed a good job elsewhere, and folded up their tent. The Labor Department issued a contract to another firm to provide clerical services, retaining one Creighton logistics person who wanted to stay on (eventually landing himself a professional job elsewhere in the department). Mark Hunker soon left the agency, as did the Acting Assistant Secretary. Over the next two years, Roland Droitsch found himself reporting to four more Assistant Secretaries.

The skunkworks facility is still there. It's used primarily as a meeting center, although a few people reside temporarily in the facility. Droitsch and Jones recently moved more workstations into the open space, as much to protect the space as anything else. Droitsch made a run at sharing the space on a contract basis with other organizations, hoping to use the acquired funds to sponsor other Department of Labor teams in the skunkworks, but that plan was quickly squelched.

The space is not wholly unproductive—several significant initiatives have been born there, such as the Department of Labor web site. Droitsch and Jones championed the need for a web site, and used a team approach to develop its design, agree on how the site would be staffed, and get it on-line. It's now up to one million hits per year, with two to three full time staff people. A substance abuse program for small businesses and trade associations was also incubated in the facility, which continues to be booked regularly for meetings.

Lessons Learned

In postmortems with Labor Department staff it appears that the skunkworks's woes were the result of much larger management issues. The staff workers report that they can recall no administration where there has been such a sharp split between the political appointees and civil service staff. Although Secretary Reich preached empowerment, many report that "we were empowered to do what they told us." Teams that began to work together effectively and make decisions were often second-guessed by the political appointees, thus undermining the team's effectiveness. The entrenched bureaucracy played its role as well. Close observers suggest that most parts of the organization never really let their representatives on skunkworks teams make decisions on their behalf. The team in the skunkworks would hammer out an approach, and the established bureaucracies would begin their battles to overturn it. Reich didn't put a stop to this, and his political staff didn't understand why it mattered—they were too busy trying to overrule the decision themselves.

There's also been a constant revolving door, with a steady stream of management changes that has left pockets of chaos throughout the organization. It doesn't help any that the appointment of Alexis Hermann, designated to replace Bob Reich, is still held up in partisan bickering between the Republican Congress and the Democratic White House.

Roland Droitsch now believes that the handwriting was probably on the wall when he asked for a $300,000 budget and was told he would have only $10,000. Bob Reich was known as a warm person and an exciting leader—but he was very mercurial. He would grow very enthusiastic about a project like the skunkworks, but by the time it was a reality, his enthusiasms had moved on. Droitsch thinks that the Assistant Secretary was trying to send a signal that "This is just the secretary's toy, don't take it too seriously." The only problem was that Droitsch really believed in the potential of the skunkworks—and he almost made it work against all odds.

There are lessons to be learned from the Department of Labor skunkworks that are universal in all organizations:

○ *Innovation programs need broader support than just the CEO.* Major shifts in organizational culture take about five years—few CEOs last that long. Unless the CEO builds support for the change throughout management, the program may die the day the CEO walks out the door.

○ *Innovative programs need to be put in the context of a larger organizational strategy.* When the skunkworks was established, the Department of Labor had no history of working in teams. It had little history of using facilitators, or of using group process techniques. It had no history of empowering decision making for its own managers, let alone teams. The result was that people who considered bringing teams into the skunkworks had no context for evaluating what it could do for them. (It became an even harder sell when a political appointee who had no background in these fields was put in charge.) For the skunkworks to work, it had to be part of a much larger, systematic change program. Labor Department management had the rhetoric of culture change, but the reality was in constant contradiction to the rhetoric. The irony is that for the few short months that the skunkworks offered a full-blown program, it did work for the teams in residency.

○ *A small version of the total concept is better than a watered down version for more people.* The Labor Department spent hundreds of thousands of dollars getting the skunkworks ready, then couldn't find the funds to operate it the way it needed to be operated. There's no magic formula, but experience suggests that many times it is wise to do a pilot study that demonstrates the entire innovation, critique it, revise it, and retest it, before pushing it out to the larger organization. The pilot study is not just a test of the concept, it's also a way to build a base of support and have evidence to support use of the innovation with a larger audience. The alternative, of course, is a situation like the Silicon Junction intranet, where the innovation started happening throughout the organization, and management was bright enough to simply provide enabling tools and channel it into productive purposes.

Notes

1. These statistics are taken from Patrick Flanigan, "Silicon Graphics Raises the Standard," *Telecommunications* (January 1997, p. S7:S25).
2. Ibid, p. S10
3. Claremont Technology Group Inc., *Claremont Intranet Study; Impact on Silicon Graphics* (September 1996).
4. Internal report provided by Silicon Graphics, Inc.
5. Personal interview with Lori-Leanne Parris (April 18, 1997).
6. Doug Hall with David Wecker, *Jump Start Your Brain* (New York: Warner Books, 1995).
7. MG Taylor Corporation, *Discover the Genius in Your Organization* (Hilton Head, South Carolina: MG Taylor, Draft version 4.0, 1997).
8. Gayle Pergamit and Chris Peterson, *Leaping the Abyss: Putting Group Genius to Work* (in press). © 1997 by Gayle Pergamit and Chris Peterson; www.pergamit.com.
9. The Scan, Focus, Act model was developed by Frank Burns and Linda Nelson, copyright 1983, MetaSystems Design Group, Arlington Virginia.
10. Pergamit and Peterson, p. 61.
11. Ibid., p. 209.
12. The AEDC story is from a personal interview with Colonel Rutley on April 23, 1997, as well as from material taken from Pergamit and Peterson. The opinions expressed are Colonel Rutley's, and are not the official position of the U.S. Air Force.
13. Langdon Morris, *Managing the Evolving Corporation* (New York: Van Nostrand Reinhold, 1995).

14

You Ain't
Seen Nothin' Yet

"I've just bought ten square miles of virtual reality," reported Jim Channon on the phone the other day. Channon, a leading graphic recorder and meeting facilitator, must have heard the dead silence as we tried to visualize what he meant. "We're going to construct a 50-story conference center, and I've already sold 13 floors," he said. We were beginning to understand, but it was coming slowly.

Channon's vision is of a "cyberversity." Participants will attend classes, conferences, and workshops in a facility that exists entirely in cyber-reality. They will be able to sit comfortably in their homes, observing everything on a giant wall-sized screen, moving through the cyber facility on the wheels of their computer mouse. They will be able to glide down the corridors of a virtual building, the design of which is no longer constrained by the limitations of holding up ceilings or observing the laws of gravity. Every element of the building, sound, color, light can be controlled to support any particular kind of meeting, then instantly reconfigured for another.

Participants will be able to "see" each other, although they will really be viewing each other's *avatars*, graphic representations of themselves. One person's avatar may be an actual photo, another's avatar may be the image of a mythic beast or a comic-book character. In fact, the creation of custom-designed avatars will become a major industry, with leading avatar designers enjoying celebrity status.

One advantage of dealing with avatars is that you can glide up to any one of them, click on your mouse, and pull up a short bio before you begin talking. Or you can simply relate to what you see, with the advantage that your perceptions are not influenced by issues of gender, race, or physical characteristics. The disadvantage, of course, is that what you see may not be what you get.

The walls of the rooms are like web sites. If there's anything on them that looks interesting, you just click on it, and you can gain access to multiple layers of information about the object or topics. Group graphics don't have to be static images, but can be animated with all the features of a 3-D movie. Also, avatars don't get tired, so you don't have to provide tables and chairs.

All of this might sound totally fantastic, but Channon says he's already sold thirteen floors to major corporations. In a world where the personal computer is still less than 20 years old, and the World Wide Web is about three, Channon's vision may not be that far off.

Throughout this book, we have provided a glimpse of what the future may be like. One problem with writing a book like this is that the reality so quickly overruns our ability to imagine the possibilities. The leading technologists tell us that in the very short term, things won't change as much as we think they're going to. But in the long term, they'll change a lot more than we can imagine.

We're convinced certain basics will remain:

○ The real issue is collaboration; technology is simply a valuable tool for helping to bring it about.
○ The magic is in the synthesis of all the components of collaboration—corporate culture, technology, group process, and interactive facilities (virtual or otherwise).
○ The real payoff from collaborative technology will come when we invent whole new ways of working that we haven't even dreamed of yet—not from just doing the things we're doing now faster and better.

○ Collaboration must be managed; it's not just a by-prod-
uct, nor is it automatic just because people are connected electronically.

We hope we've helped frame some of the possibilities, and
shown how the pieces fit together. It's going to be exciting,
and it's already happening!

Index

viewing screens, 58–59
VisiCalc, 88
visual group memory, 5, 7, 73,
   77–78, 112, 152

walls and wall space
   in interactive meeting rooms,
      99, 100
   and meeting process, 73,
      76–77
   movable, 99
Walt Disney Corporation, 194
Web browsers, 55–56
WebCrawler, 56
Wharton School, 197
whiteboard/copiers, 63
whiteboards, 10, 62–66
   implementation of, 152

in interactive meeting rooms,
   100
   PC-linked, 50, 86
   in skunkworks, 102
whiteboard tables, 10
Wiener, Norbert, 12*n*
Wilms, Wellford, on teams, 97
The Wisdom of Teams
   (Katzenbach and Smith), 88
working walls, 4–6
workstations, in skunkworks,
   102–104
World Wide Web, 49, 55–57
Wright, Frank Lloyd, on
   building, 132

Yahoo!, 56